For Grace.

With love,

Yin Xi

HOME IS HERE

a memoir

Yin Xzi Ho

何 吟 曦

◆ FriesenPress

Suite 300 - 990 Fort St
Victoria, BC, V8V 3K2
Canada

www.friesenpress.com

ISBN
978-1-03-910628-4 (Hardcover)
978-1-03-910627-7 (Paperback)
978-1-03-910629-1 (eBook)

1. BIOGRAPHY & AUTOBIOGRAPHY, PERSONAL MEMOIRS

Distributed to the trade by The Ingram Book Company

TABLE OF CONTENTS

ACKNOWLEDGEMENTS

Growing up and reading the acknowledgements of every book I've ever read has given me ample time to plan what I would write in the acknowledgements of my book-to-be—a dream I've had since second grade. And yet, here I am, feeling unprepared to write this section of my book.

The names of people outnumber the names of places, but I find it helpful to remind myself that much like the phases of the moon, there are people who have waned out and people who have waxed in. And so, I render this series of acknowledgements as a permanent articulation of thanks for this point in time. The writing of this keystone would not have been possible without the following communities.

To my family—my mother, Wei Ling Poon, my father, Fendy Ho, my sisters, Tien Xzi and Ro Xzi—I am so grateful. Thank you for always being my home, thank you for always being family, thank you for your care, your kindness, for your patience and mindfulness, for the laughter, the inspiration, and for answering my inane questions as I wrote this book—I am always and endlessly grateful.

To my Quest humans—Daniela J., Minouka K., Matilda G., Paige W., Shuyu W., Dafny M., Maya H-L., Vasi U., Jacob T., Fiona H., Zoe F., Keane H., Niall H., Sahar T., and Hannah R. as an honorary student—thank you for being gentle, thank you for being curious, thank you for being here.

To the Matthews-de Groot abode—Asia, Rueben, Lowell, and Zevon—thank you for giving me a home when I needed it most and changing my life, forever.

To the Bracko Beans—Jamie H., Bea C., Lucie B., Enoch and Ethan K-S., and Cael G.—thank you for being there in the end, taking me to adventures, letting me have my rituals, and working beside me even when I am far away in my own head.

To my Bhutan family—Alaina P., Ann C., Ben W., Bhuwan K., Brendan Z., Hannah L., Lacey C., Nick B., Oscar G., Rachel S., Sam P., Tandin S., Tenzin N., Tori M., and Weymar O.—thank you for becoming home in a faraway place; what else were we going to do?

To my mentor—Fei Shi—thank you for your endless support.

To my editors and beta readers—Phil C., Emma H., Lucie B., Niall H., Paige W., Diane M., Maya H-L., Jacob T., Hannah R., Lacey C., and Minouka K.—thank you for catching the gaps, thank you for noting the joy.

To the countless moving and thought-provoking conversations about everything by the light of the sun and the depth of the moon: Zoe (thank you for the words, for the stories, for the generations of knowledge and home), Minouka (thank you for the quiet, for the walks, for the slow-cooked, homemade food), Lacey (thank you for being a home, for letting me see yours, for coming to see mine, for being a soulmate, and an adventure buddy), Wei Qian (thank you for childhood, for the late night novel writing—"just write it!"—for unwavering encouragement, and the playground escapades), and Jamie (thank you for seeing me, and being patient, thank you for waiting until I have the words).

To myself of the past, thank you for writing, for recording. To myself of the present, thank you for writing, for remembering. To myself of the future, thank you for writing, for becoming.

To my places—thank you for being heavy, for being light, for being near and far, for teaching, for listening, for the most joyous of times to the most beautiful griefs.

To my readers—I hope you read this and feel as if you are coming home; I hope you read this and know that this is my way of coming home to you.

Thank you all for reminding me that I belong here, always. You are all woven into everything I do—I cannot say it often enough, though I try and will keep trying: thank you.

With love,
Yin Xzi

"Home is here... is a bold statement.
It is applicable to each and every poem, story, anecdote,
wondering, searching, yearning,
connecting, disconnecting page of your book.
And it answers your question."

— Phil Clark

TIMELINE

- **1998–2004: MALAYSIA**
  - December 1998: I am born in Kuala Lumpur, Malaysia.
  - 1998–2004: My family lives in Sungai Buloh, Malaysia.
  - April 2001: Tien Xzi is born.
  - June 2003: Ro Xzi is born.

- **2004–2014: CHINA**
  - December 2004: My family moves to Guangzhou, China.
  - January 2005: We live in Golden Lake, a neighborhood in the Baiyun District, near Guangzhou.
  - 2006–2008: We live in Tower 11 in Grandview Garden, a neighborhood on Ersha Island in Guangzhou.
  - 2008–2013: We live in Tower 7 in Grandview Garden.
  - 2013–July 2014: We live in Dragon Pearl, the neighborhood adjacent to Grandview Garden.

- **2014–2017: MALAYSIA**
  - July 2014: We move back to Sungai Buloh, Malaysia, into my childhood home.
  - January 2015–2017: We move to our new house in Sungai Buloh (which my family currently resides in).

- **2017–2019: CANADA**
  - August 2017: I move onto my university campus in Squamish, British Columbia, Canada.
  - December 2017: I fly home to Malaysia for two and a half weeks.
  - January 2018: I fly home to Squamish.

- **2019: CANADA, MALAYSIA, BHUTAN, MYANMAR, AUSTRALIA**
  - May 2019: I fly home to Malaysia and live in Sungai Buloh.
  - July 2019: I fly to Thimphu, Bhutan, by means of Thailand, and live on another university campus.
  - Start of December 2019: We—my friends and I—leave Bhutan to travel through Thailand and Myanmar.
  - Mid-December 2019: I am home in Malaysia for two weeks.
  - End of December 2019: I fly to Australia.

- **2020: AUSTRALIA, MALAYSIA, CANADA**
  - January 2020: I live in Australia in a van with Lacey for nineteen days before flying home to Malaysia for Chinese New Year.
  - February 2020: I return to Squamish.
  - End of March 2020: I move off campus and into a home with a family in the Garibaldi Highlands, a neighborhood in Squamish.
  - End of August 2020 to present: Move from the Highlands to Brackendale, another neighborhood in Squamish, in a house with peers.

INTRODUCTION

There is a far lengthier 'Afterword' that lies at the end of this book. It delves more specifically into the logic behind each section of this memoir and my writing process, but I urge you to read that after reading the memoir itself. This is so that the journey set before you has the space and time to unfold in your mind. The memoir begins with me at the age of five, newly moved to China. The memoir closes with me at twenty-one, living in Canada. What unfolds in-between is a prolonged, tender, curious, and bittersweet exploration of asking where I come from, of asking where I call home, of asking where I belong.

My goals in writing this memoir were as follows: to create a space where I can reclaim a narrative for myself, to explore the contradictions and joys of growing through multiple countries, and to contextualize and complicate the definition of belonging. My goals were informed by the scholarship I read about Southeast Asian literature and wider understandings of belonging. *Home is Here* is not a passive receptacle for my many experiences. Rather, my memoir is actively a site of investigation into the logics of belonging as affected by nationality, gender, and identity. I hope to offer some insight into the transnational experiences of (Chinese-)Malaysians in the twenty-first century.

As you read, I invite you to think upon the questions: *Do I belong? Where do I come from? Where do I call home? How do I know this?*

CHINA

何吟曦

In kindergarten, I write my name: *Ho Yin Xzi*.
It is the literal translation of my name from Mandarin to English.
My teacher frets over me—she is a cloud of heavy perfume
and long light-colored hair.
She tells me: *"Your name is Yin Xzi Ho."*

I swing my own long black hair across my face,
evading her eyes. I murmur an understanding.
Secretly, I write *Ho Yin Xzi* in large letters on the inside of
    my notebook.
It is the first rebellion. I keep it to myself.

I write my name at the top of my homework: *Ho Yin Xzi*.
My name flows from my math worksheet onto the table repeatedly,
where it is seen and I am caught—made to stay inside
    during recess—
to clean it up and write down the rearrangement.

A furious, quiet anger builds inside me as I erase lead from the
    table top.
My teacher gives me a sheet of lined paper, and ample time.
Framed by red and blue lines, my new name appears:
Yin Xzi Ho. Yin Xzi Ho. Yin Xzi Ho.

This new American way puts me first, before my family.
This new way places me farther—makes me forget, a little
the beauty of my name
and the story behind it.

In Mandarin, my name is 何吟曦.[1]
The character that is unique to me—吟—is placed
in the middle, held and surrounded by my family—何,
and the character that I share with my sisters—曦.

In Mandarin, my name—吟曦
translates roughly to "an ancient song or chant",
and "the first light of dawn".
In English, I paraphrase this into "poetic sunrise".

Years later, I write my name: *Yin Xzi Ho.*
Years later, I remember that my name
doesn't have to stand alone.
Underneath, I write 何吟曦.

....

1   Hé yín xī: Ho Yin Xzi

C-17

I revisit this house through kaleidoscopic lenses. It is the first place we live in. The staircase trails upward through my imagination for hours, and my room is a large space that I can never quite fill, not even a decade and a half later.

The house has been distorted by traveling through the recesses of my brain. Rooms don't stay in place as I walk in through the large wooden front doors and past the living room. The kitchen is an indecipherable mass of beige and light. My parents' room—which they often shared with my sisters—stretches far away from me, down the hall. The distance between my room and theirs has been exaggerated over the years, with the hallway carpet unrolling a bit farther with every step.

I know now that the exaggerated size of the house comes from how small I was when we lived there. Despite the vagueness of the house itself I have precious, vivid, one-off memories that flare brightly. Rarely do I bring myself to recall these; I am worried that dredging them up would cause them to fade and warp.

Changes to these memories have been slow, with time and inconsistent retellings aggregating over time to build up a film that I now squint through in order to recall the past.

To write it all down now—an ocean and sixteen years away—is a difficult act of preservation. The journey begins as it always does—by learning to ride a bike.

*   *   *

In the distance, I watch my father teach me how to ride a bike on the road outside of C-17. The bike is red, and the road is paved with large flat cobblestones. Underneath me, the bike is a strange extension of my limbs—one made of stiffer material and an innate desire to roll smoothly forwards. I hesitate, fingers pumping the brakes and feet dropping to the floor. The training wheels and my father's hands catch me before I hit the curb.

The familiar vessel that is me has been thwarted. Rubber wheels touch the curve of the earth instead of the soles of my feet. My hands stop movement instead of swinging in time with my legs. Even my head is doubled in size with the "safety-first" helmet buckled on.

Days of practice and weeks of careful encouragement later, my father is not there to watch me ride my bike down the hill for the first time. The world tilts precariously downwards. The bottom of the hill rushes to meet me and pain reminds me of that which is my body and that which is my bike.

Sketched over the feel of being suddenly airborne and then violently grounded is the knowledge that tonight I will yet again be made to sleep alone.

My mother tends to my scrapes, and when my father comes home, the heroic nature of my great bike tragedy is acknowledged. I hold onto the feeling of togetherness for as long as I can, wincing when I step and feigning a dependency that matches the level of my youngest sister.

From a distance, I watch my parents put me to bed. Having my own room at the end of the hall is an honor, or so my new American friends tell me. My parents assure me that I can handle it, that I am old enough, that the house is big enough. I put on a brave face and am inwardly envious of my sisters, still small enough to sleep curled up by my parents in their bed.

I fight the whole process, from toothbrushing to the actual act of falling asleep. But the day has exhausted me, and my eyes slip closed.

Eventually, the nightmares arrive to awaken me, and before I am truly alert, my mouth is open and crying. It is a plea for someone in the house to wake up and carry me to a space I feel safe enough to fall asleep in. Namely, it is a call to action for either my parents or my *ayi*[2]

---

2   阿姨 (āyí): "aunt" and also a familial way of referring to maids

downstairs to wake up and bring me to my parents' room, where my younger sisters sleep soundly by my mom and dad.

Reunited, I fall asleep soundly to the rise and fall rhythms of my family.

汤圆

Food is made to be shared, my 大舅婆[3] tells me, from the process of making food to the eating of it.

Making food together is a time to tell stories and a time to forge new ones to tell the next time the dish gets made.

The dish whose process sits closest to my heart is 汤圆,[4] a dessert eaten during winter solstice. Literally translated, the name of the dish means "round soup," which paints a decently accurate picture of the dish itself: balls of colored glutinous rice flour eaten with a sweet and warm ginger soup. The glutinous rice flour balls themselves can be filled with a black sesame or red bean paste to add additional flavor or texture, though most of the homemade tang yuan I have had growing up skips this step.

*　*　*

My 大舅婆 and 大舅公[5] come and visit us one December to experience the novelty of a mild winter. It is December 21, and we are making tang yuan.

We gather around our kitchen table, and my great aunt measures out a heaping of glutinous rice flour. She teaches us how to color the flour with the littlest bits of pandan water, or sweet potato, or dragonfruit.

I press together my hands and form the smallest of balls, rolling the cool dough between my palms. They leave light-colored circles—pink and orange and green. The kitchen grows warm as we shape the dessert, as we boil water to cook the tang yuan and slice up ginger to make the accompanying sweet soup.

---

3   Dà jiù pó: great aunt
4   Tāng yuán: known in English as *tang yuan*
5   Dà jiù gōng: great uncle

It takes hours, and by the time the tang yuan is ready, my stomach is grumbling. We carry out bowls and the pots and set them on the table. My mother ladles a rainbow into our bowls, then pours the hot and sweet ginger soup over it all. We exclaim over the sweetness in our mouths, at the warmth in our bodies. My glasses fog in the cool winter air as I chew through the soft, doughy texture of the dessert.

*　　*　　*

Years later, for my twenty-first birthday, my mother, my sister, and I replicate the process. The recipe for tang yuan is not one that I know how to articulate in culinary terms. I do not have the words to describe how the dough feels when it is ready to be broken up and rolled into spheres—this recipe is one I know instinctively through my hands and my mouth.

My ability to know when the balls are cooked (they dance to the top of the pot), to know that you should cook the tang yuan in plain boiling water and douse it in cold before you serve it with the soup is all knowledge embedded in me from making the dish over and over again with my mother.

My 大舅婆 knows that I adore tang yuan, and on the occasions in which I return home to Malaysia, she makes it especially for me, even if it isn't December 21. It is a demonstration of love and of care that I am all too lucky to have. Having tang yuan made for me and the process of making it with others is an act that tells me that I am home: here, you are home.

Ersha Island

The island has been covered with blooming orchid trees—
their flowers are a series of delicate purples, bruised pinks, and
    sunset-like veins.
I collect an armful after heavy spring rains.
Armed with colored pencils, I take to coloring the awkwardly
    graceful shapes
with all the intensity a fourth grader can muster.

The first one blooms—
lilac lipstick clumsily applied.
The second is a violet butterfly crashing into the page.
A third flutters open as an iris-colored eye.

The house fills with the sweet scent of unfurling white jade orchids
and my plum-colored fingers leave prints on the walls by the stairs.
Year after year, I grow with the trees and my relatives say
that I have bloomed as beautifully as the flowers themselves.

Six years later, the air of house is cut with heavy folds of air
    that smell
like butter, brown sugar, and dark chocolate—
This time, armed with words, I take to planting the delicate beauty
on the page in a way that protects them for years.

Originally written May 2016

中秋节

In China, we place the moon on par with the sun—its presence is the thing with which years are organized, with which days are given meaning. The phases of the moon, as it waxes and wanes, tell stories of blooming trees and of the tides that greet the fishermen as they row out to meet the sea.

The moon is powerful, and kind, and gentle. Its light makes things soft and invites the telling of secrets that are too fragile to be told by the full light of day. Stories surrounding the moon have taught me that the moon is more than a big rock that rotates around the earth—the moon is a being that has seen the rise and fall of dynasties. The moon is a being that doesn't need to be understood. All we need to do, all we can do as humans, is tell the stories of the moon and teach others about the rituals that surround it.

At the end of summer, as the moon waxes into fullness, the air comes alive with bustling activity. Street-side stalls and stores alike swell full with the sweet scent of mooncakes. The golden surface of the cakes beckon customers to lean closer with intricate designs of embossed flowers and vines.

Each night, the silver coin in the sky grows a little larger; its light is made a little sharper by cooling air.

It is the beginning of autumn and so it is time for 中秋节[6]—the smell of roasted chestnuts on crisp air and the crunch of dry leaves underfoot. My mother buys paper lanterns in anticipation for the family dinner we will have on the night of the festival. The paper bundle is a tight series of colors—there is yellow and pink and green.

In China, far away from our relatives, we gather instead with the people that we can share a roof with. The day the sun is set to

---

6   Zhōng qiū jié: Mid-Autumn Festival

welcome the full moon, we crowd into the biggest of our aunties'[7] houses. The dinner is filled with round foods, fall mushrooms, and lotus root soup. We are all dressed in clothes that mark a special occasion—not our best but enough to mark that it is an occasion. The adults shoo us away so that they can chatter and play *mahjong*. We kids play long complicated games of hide and seek, watching the growing darkness with eager anticipation.

Sugar-filled dinner drinks fuel our actions, and when we tire of hide and seek, we gather around the *mahjong* table, listening to the clatter of tiles wash over the felt. The game itself is indecipherable, but our parents' joy is clear as they exchange jibes and laughter.

When night settles in, the lanterns are pulled out and we clamor for our favorites—the one that unfolds into a yellow oval, the light purple one with flowers printed across its many faces. Carefully, we set candles in the middle and walk around the neighborhood with our bobbing lights, faces illuminated both by the warmth carried by our hands and the moon.

The walk ends when our candles are snuffed out by the wind or have burnt themselves down to the wick. We crowd back into the house with glee, knowing the sweet dessert about to come our way.

Our parents bring the mooncakes out in a grand ceremony—each family proclaiming the set that they brought as the best. We *ooh* and *ahh* over each one, stomachs rumbling. Soon (but never soon enough) the packaging is torn open and the mooncake released from its plastic container and placed on a plate. We count off the number of heads in the room, and the knife descends, splitting the mooncake into twenty or thirty miniscule pieces. The single salted yolk crumbles into golden dust at the edge of everyone's plates.

---

7   It is a custom to refer to close family friends as "aunties" or "uncles."

家

As a family, we live on Ersha Island.
This is where we have our bedrooms
and my mother's inherited *wok*.
And when we go back to Malaysia for Chinese New Year,
this is where we pack big boxes of things:
mandarin oranges and *Lao Gan Ma*,[8]
mooncakes and *rou gan*.[9]

We bring these things home
to our aunts, uncles, cousins,
and for my grandmother who loves the taste of chili oil.
We bring back boxes full of things we can only find in China.

But Ersha Island is also where we return with boxes full
of spices for curries and packets of herbs to cook with.
We smuggle in heaps of baby milk formula, milo, and
Hup Seng Cream Cracker packets by the dozens.
These things we bring back for ourselves.
They are our late night comfort drinks,
our to-remember-Malaysia by foods.
This is where we talk about going home for Chinese New Year,
even though here, we are already always in our house,
in our 家 with our 家.[10]

---

8   老干妈 (lǎo gàn mā): a brand of chili sauces
9   肉干 (ròu gān): a Chinese salty-sweet dried meat, also known as bakkwa
10 Jiā: a word used interchangeably to refer to home/house/family

If a 家 is a family under one roof—宀.[11]
Can you render one under two?
Is there another word, another character,
another place by which I can understand why it is
that, as a family, we live here?
Here in a place that we must always travel away from
to go home again.

11 Mián: a radical that means roof

Grandview Garden

Up in the branches of our favorite mango tree—
the one that has seen our changeover of friends,
as people move to and from our home—
Wei Qian and I make a neighborhood of our own.

It looks like this one, with apartment buildings
and green spaces and playgrounds.
It's studded with the amber-colored buds of mango trees.
And when the heavy spring rains arrive,
the neighborhood of white-tiled apartments and brick paths
catch and press the blossoms against the floor and the rising heat of
    the earth
to turn the heavy and humid air into a sea of mangoes too.

But here—here in the neighborhood that we've imagined—
we know everyone's name.
We've chosen our friends
and the teachers who encourage us to follow our passions.
The branches we sit and swing, amongst waxy leaves,
are familiar with us too.

Our families live here too, of course,
and this mango tree.
There are tiny pieces of our schools scattered throughout
as a staircase or two,
the big library of light and many favorite books—
the neighborhood is filled with all that we recognize as home.

In this neighborhood, there is a certain sort of stability—
a steadiness that doesn't exist in international schools—
that weather remains perfect, though the definition of that varies.
Up in the mango tree, we dance and sway with typhoon winds.

Together, we decide:
any mandate from us becomes law,
whatever we say becomes truth—
but what we mean, mostly, is
we hope you stay.

Dragon Pearl

"It's time for us to go."

My dad's voice catches my chin and pulls it upwards. I hold my breath, unsure whether to scramble back up to my bedroom and feign sleep or to remain where I am in the living room. I wait for a cue to tell me what to do.

If my family were to be a musical ensemble, we would be the kind that never gets to choose the music we play. My dad would be first violin and my mom, the second—softer and meant to play the harmony. My sisters and I would alternate through the viola, cello, and double bass. The individual instruments we hold are irrelevant—we exist to anchor the rhythm of the piece. If we are lucky, we would be given the chance to play a melody. But for the most part, we would be expected to be consistent, quiet, and steady—as I had been for fifteen years. I find a certain sort of comfort in my role—I know my part, and I play it well.

The soft creak of wood on the second floor tells me that my dad has moved into the bathroom. I allow myself to exhale and tell myself not to cry. Tears, my father was fond of telling me, are a sign of weakness. And you, the saying implied, are not weak.

Silence resettles itself around the contours of the second floor. My mother and sisters are still asleep. As I breathe, I lean into the familiar air of our Dragon Pearl apartment. After a year of growing into it, today is the last day I get to call it home.

I had woken up that morning hours before the birds had started calling and brushed my teeth quietly in the dim light coming through the bathroom window. My breath caught at the softest of noises—the whine of the tap, the churning flush of the toilet. I waited for the bones of the house to settle before moving again. Quietly, I slipped out of the bathroom, through the cavernous and bare hallway, past the airy landing, and down the spiraling marble stairs into the living room—and here, I stand, waiting.

The burble of water rising through the pipes marks the beginning of my dad's long morning routine. I listen for a while, knowing the rhythms of the house and the people within it.

My chest swells with the desire to memorize every lilting melody.

My gaze wanders across the largely empty living room, taking in the curtainless windows and the adjoining dining room—seeking a reason to stay. My eyes catch on my white and neon green roller-blades, which lean against a cardboard box labeled "Dining Room." I survey them from a distance, twisting my toes against the cool floor. The rollerblades' fluorescent detailing had withstood a test of eleven months spent shut in the dark airless corners of the cupboard under the stairs. A tiny tendril of guilt snakes through me.

The rollerblades have belonged to me for five years—half of my lifetime spent in China. I could feel the rattle of my bones as my muscles remembered learning to rollerblade. My mom had held my hand as I rolled, tentatively, across the bumpy, textured pavement that weaves across Ersha Island. Now, however, there is no hand holding—today's particular movement would have to be learned on my own.

Doors open upstairs—my mom and my sisters wandering out of their rooms—and it propels me into the kitchen. The sounds of my family waking up fills the air around me like a rising tide, and I let myself be pulled along in one last song and dance.

Absent-mindedly, I pull open the cupboard door for our peanut butter and jam, and find an empty, gaping shelf looking back at me. My arm convulses and I yank myself away from the shelves before my instinctive reaction to lash out takes over. I close my eyes and inhale, shakily, slowly. *Don't you dare cry.* The last loaf of bread sits on the counter next to the last bits of Nutella.

It has been time to go for weeks now. It began with the arrival of percussive sounds—the assembling of cardboard boxes, the stuffing of bubble wrap, the ripping of packing tape. Each roll of a carpet, and boxing of objects pulled us a little closer to the unmaking of our final apartment in Guangzhou, China. Five homes in fifteen years should have made me fluent in the phenomenon of movement to pre-planned music, but today, I am finding that my feet still stumble with unwelcome staccato. My family bustles into the kitchen, and the air fills with tremulous breathing. I draw air only into the highest part of my chest—releasing slowly—as if I fear that breathing too deeply would prompt me to float away.

My family drinks from cups before rinsing, drying, and placing them carefully into a box labeled "Kitchen." I follow suit, moving sluggishly, caught in my own thoughts. If they notice my sullen teenage behavior, they choose not to comment. My shoulders sag with relief as my parents disappear back upstairs to sort the last of their clothes. My sisters eventually trail up behind them.

Holding my breath, I wander back out into the living room. I go back to watching my rollerblades.

"We're leaving soon," my dad calls from his room. His voice rings, deep and unflinching, through the house. It sounds practiced. There is enough empty space in the house now for his voice to echo.

Cotton pulls itself over my ears, blocking out the note of sadness that winds its way through my dad's words. Dwelling too deeply on how he would miss China makes it hard for me to be angry at him. I shove the feeling deep into my stomach.

Heart fluttering in my chest, I move quickly, unsteadily to my rollerblades. I pull them on, tugging at the straps and teasing my feet in.

They fit.

For a moment, I sit, memorizing the feel of them on my feet. The soles are worn with little hollows for my toes and valleys for my heels.

I push myself up, and outside of my own volition, the tilt of the floor pushes me towards the dining room. A smile interrupts my face as I push my right leg back and almost immediately, my left leg skids too far forwards. I catch myself and hold still, trying to figure out how to reallocate my weight. I center my hips, stick my arms out to my sides, and begin where I started, with my feet held tight and parallel and my head high—a modified second position in ballet. My smile stretches a little larger as a giddy happiness winds its way up my torso.

I imagine myself in the hallway upstairs. Though empty now, I imagine the heavy bookshelves that had stood guard every night outside our bedrooms are there again. I nose along the hallway and bid a last, wordless goodbye.

I had volunteered to pack all the books alone and had pushed my dad forcefully aside when his hands reached in to help.

I had swept the last row of books off the shelf and caused them to cascade down, with one of them hitting my foot. Tears welled up in my eyes, and an irrational *don't you dare cry* flitted through my head. My sisters were in their bedroom just off their hallway, murmuring about their stuffed animals. I had to maintain the rhythm. Nothing was wrong.

I bit my tongue and apologized to the shelves for tearing out all they had held and protected.

I had maintained the alphabetical-organization-by-last name as I packed the books away, but later found that the books had been reorganized, optimized instead for space. My mother's careful, attentive packing tightened my shoulders, tearing me between the possibility of lashing out at her for changing something I loved dearly and thanking her. A stack of books sat to the side, awaiting my decision—to donate or to pack. I shoved them haphazardly into the remaining empty spaces, determined not to leave them behind.

This move was different from the last two, where each home had been within walking distance. There wasn't going to be the chance for me to sprint back, out of breath, to pull one last forgotten object out from under my bed and carry it tenderly to the new house.

Anything forgotten in this round would be permanently, irrevocably left behind. I was not going to be leaving anything behind.

"It's time for us to go," my mom calls from the landing on the second floor. She sounded annoyingly chipper, like she was trying to pep talk us all.

My smile slips away as my knees sink towards the ground. I had been skating circles around the living room, imagining things as they had been upstairs, and now my eyebrows furrowed at the interruption.

"It's time for us to go," my mom calls again, suddenly on the staircase, dressed in a polyester purple shirt and a pair of pink batik shorts. They had white hibiscuses painted onto them. They were the kind of shorts that tourists buy when they're on vacation in Malaysia and want to come away showing that they've truly engaged with the culture. My sisters and I would make fun of the *gweilo*[12] that would try them on, uncomfortably engaging the small connection we had to our country of birth by teasing those who appeared to belong less than we did. But it was unfair to see my mom in this light—batik is a part of her that she had tried to share with us. We have batik sarongs and dresses tailor-made for us every summer. Sometimes, the clothes made me feel more like a tourist and less like a Malaysian.

The air inside me curdles. My gaze swings back down to the slide of beige marble.

"I. Don't. Care."

My mother sighs and makes her way down the staircase, used to my tiny deviations from the written music. The soles of her feet slapping the stairs sound like the rip of packing tape.

I close my eyes, splaying my hands out to watch for pieces of furniture as I continue to skate. When only air hits me, I remember— everything has been Tetris-stacked into the back of a moving van. My chest caves once more.

12 Cantonese for "foreigner"

With my eyes still shut, I continue sliding across the floor, imagining the couch and the coffee table, and the dining table and the ornate cupboard that had held wines and tea and statues of the Buddha. The large pieces of furniture had acted as active family members, joining our dinner conversations and watching TV with us. Now they were stifled in several layers of heavy cloth, waiting to begin a five-month journey by sea to the new empty house.

I roll into where the dining table once stood and, with my back to my mom, open my eyes.

White jade orchid and ficus bonsai trees sway outside. I squint against their scatter of gold sunlight and listen to the thud of my heart. My mother inhales, testing the air around me, trying to figure out how tight it is.

"Do you want to keep them?"

I didn't answer. Instead, my eyes drop, traitorously, from the trees of the island down to my rollerblades. The thudding of my heart speeds up as I tell myself not to cry. *Don't you dare cry.* Instead, I start moving again, farther away from my mom.

The corner of the room forces a sharp turn. My hair swings into my face and blinds me.

My mom stands at the bottom of the staircase, with her hands on her hips. It is a posture of sharp angles—a bristling fortress that protects herself and makes it easier for me to want to demolish the walls.

"Do you want to take them or not?"

I watch the dust bunnies churn against the white rubber wheels of my rollerblades and bite back the answer that comes rushing up, surprising me with its heat and bile. The words I want to weaponize confuse me. I want to retort that there isn't a future in Malaysia—that I can't see myself rollerblading there, that I don't want to go—I want to stay here. But . . . the stack of books and my unpacked rollerblades come to mind. I don't want to be left behind either.

I wonder what would have happened had I confessed this, if I had skated over to my mom and hugged her, jutting elbows and all. I wonder if she would have cried too—for the upcoming loss of friends, of home. These were untested waters for the both of us—me delaying something as large and inevitable as the move. In this symphony, I was the out-of-time and novice player.

I clench my jaw so hard it aches.

Don't you dare cry.

During the first orchestrated move from Kuala Lumpur, Malaysia, to Guangzhou, China, I was only a little older than five and content to play whatever instrument was put in my hands. My only insistence was that I be allowed to bring my teddy bear and my sisters along. I had been terrified that we would leave my sisters behind to fend for themselves alone in the Sungai Buloh house with its steep wooden staircase.

Now, at fifteen, I understand a little more about the musical theory behind moving. I know about the financial time signature that set the pace of the piece, and that we have no choice in leaving this time around. I know that the first move from Malaysia to China had been for our education, for a better future.

Now though, I can tell that something has shifted—I am almost as tall as my mom—I have managed to pull the violin out of her hands. Now that I have, I am not sure what to do. I've never taken a solo before.

The wheels of my rollerblades spin beneath me.

At this moment, I want to ask the questions that have paralyzed me in bed every night since I was told that we would move back to Malaysia. My mind begins sentences that never make it to my mouth. Fragments of questions, of pleas, of explanations, and apologies.

"We can pack them and go," she says, voice softer. I don't look at her. Everything feels hot and blurred. I look at the floor. At the stupid cardboard boxes. At the stupid yellow-orange packing tape that smells like burnt plastic.

My esophagus squeezes air out of my body, and I gasp involuntarily and feel a hot bullet slide down my face.

Don't you dare cry. My sisters are relying on me to carry the beat. I cannot cry.

I try as hard as I can to will the tear back. It doesn't work. (It never does.) I hold myself as still as I can even as I roll, smoothly, in the direction of the living room. Any movement would have betrayed me.

The even sweep of the wheel against the floor reminds me of a plane's take-off from the runway. A crescendo of noise from pianissimo to a fortissimo that rattles your teeth. I imagine being able to see the neighborhoods we have lived in from above. The tennis courts reduced to little squares of green the size of my pinky nails. The playgrounds hidden by mango trees, the glitter of Pearl River.

I want to tell my mom about the song "Airplanes" by B.O.B., which renders the nighttime flight path of planes in the form of shooting stars. I want to tell her how my sisters and I would sing it in Malaysia whenever we saw an airplane fly overhead at night. I want to tell her that we only used this song for the biggest of wishes. That as we sing the lyrics, our entire bodies would hope and beg and ache for what we hid underneath the words.

I want to tell her that I used to use the song to wish for Gong Gong's[13] cancer to go into remission. I want to tell her that, recently, I have been wasting my wishes on staying here.

But I don't. Instead I tell her, *"Fine."*

The word is heavy and hollow. My mouth barely moves, and I still don't meet her eyes. Her gaze is trained on me, though. I can feel it settle in the hollow of my collarbone. I focus on carving round circles into the floor, leaning into the turns.

"It's time to go."

A chill runs through my burning body. I feel like a firecracker doused in a cold bucket of water. The floor below me blurs. The air conditioner hums and shudders. It ticks to a slow stop. I draw in a long inhale and then exhale loudly. I pick my fingers up and rest

---

13 公公 (gōng gōng): grandfather on my mother's side

them gently back down on the fingerboard—resettling myself into the rhythm of my family. I know my part. I play it well.

It has been time to go for weeks now.

"*Okay,*" I said finally. "*Okay.*"

MALAYSIA

To Return

To return to Malaysia is to surrender your whole self to the tropics.
Our winter time carry-ons either include shorts and shirts to
   change into
or the necessary space to stuff our shed thermals and jackets.

My parents push trolleys with suitcases stacked as tall as I am.
I trail behind with my sisters as we head towards the exit of
   the airport.
The family that leaves the glass doors before us let in a heave of the
   night soon to hit us—
swathes of dark and damp air, crammed with the smell of
   decomposing vegetation.

The wall of humidity and heat collides into us—
The air is alive with large undulating currents that swim against me.

My skin belongs less to me and more to the breath that is
   the outside.
The boundary that defines me is suddenly less important—
if it can, the suspended water insists on becoming a part of me—
crawling down my throat and seeping into my clothes.

I am weighed with the air, and the very act of breathing
is the act of pulling, of drawing the realm of Malaysia back into me.

Thunderstorms

7:32 p.m. — 哇! 天黑了[14]
When it thunderstorms in the evenings, the sky blooms a soft,
    deep gray,
as if it is bruising right where the water falls.
Light at the edges turns a strange, flat yellow
—the last burnished bits of a setting sun consumed by rain.
When it thunderstorms in the evenings, the sky presses itself closer.
It wants to see all that I have done, and it does so by
    smothering downwards,
decreasing the distance that exists between itself and me.
In these moments, I am all the versions of me that have ever
    lived here
—a child, a teen, a young adult:
          suddenly I am six and pressing the cool metal window grate
          against my mouth as I lean against the window
          seeking lightning,

          I am sixteen and watching the clouds roil,
          pretending that the world is as angry as I am
          as the wind whips through my hair,

          I am twenty-one and in a car with my parents,
          words drowned out by the thundering
          of rain against the roof.
The flat yellow light renders me small again
and terrified of the loud noises.
It traps me like a fly caught in amber.

....
14   Wa! Tiān hēi le: "Wow! The sky is dark already."

8:27 p.m. — 打雷了[15]
We are in the middle of the thunderstorm after the sun has set
and the street lights are flaring orange dots in the night sky.
It bleeds from orange into purple before melting far into
   the horizon.
The storm sounds like standing behind a waterfall
or being surrounded by the drums of Chinese New Year.
When the thunder cracks,
         I am eight again
         and clapping my hands over my ears,
            even as my grandmother insists I leave them alone.
         She says *the drums are scaring a year's worth*
         of bad thoughts and bad luck away from me.

         I am an anxious eighteen-year-old,
            rushing out to feel the summer storm on my skin,
            newly separated from all that I call home.
In the middle of the storm, when the sky comes to greet me,
it knocks on my doors and dances at my windows.
There is nothing else to do but let it in.

---

15 Dǎ léi le: "It's thundering."

The Ocean

Here by the ocean where turtles come to lay their eggs,
and seashells tumble before lying in wait
on coarse sand to be ground down into smaller bits—
where glass drifts to be smoothed out.
This is where I have picked up my first salt stone of the summer.

Here by the ocean, I soothe myself
with the feel of grit between my toes,
and then the warm stick of salty water to my calves.

By the ocean, with its foaming reach
and hissing return,
which rests adorned by seaside pines,
purple sea pea flower,
and salt-worn swings.

Here by the ocean, I hear the slip
of words in other tongues reach quality over me
before settling down gently,
a blanket of vowels and rhythmic consonants.

By the ocean, families exclaim
in the swiftly moving darkness
over sunset shells with a hole pierced through.
The lip of the sea turns a gloaming white
in the distance.

By the ocean, there lie boats
waiting for the break of another day—
marked only by the soft light of bioluminescent plankton
and the sweep of silent fin.

Written at Pantai Teluk Mak Nik (Monica Bay), June 2019

(M)other Tongue

Mandarin is, and will forever be, my mother's tongue—in the sense that it is my (m)otherland's tongue.

As a child, I was fluent in English and Mandarin—I proudly claimed both even as strangers (with their too-loud voices and ever-searching eyes) pressed for more: *"Which one did you learn first?"*

"Both," I would struggle to explain—airless words bubbling up through my throat. *"My parents speak to my sisters and I in Mandarin, but we grew up in international schools. I'm Chinese-Malaysian, but . . . Westernized?"*

One by one, my explanations and justifications would come tumbling out. When broaching the subject of the languages I speak, I've been trained to disclose my background—that I grew up both in Malaysia and China, that I've attended international schools since the age of five, that I started learning Spanish in Grade 6. I do this because I feel the need to justify my fluency in English and my present lack of comfort in speaking Mandarin.

I stopped actively learning Mandarin when I chose to start learning Spanish while living in China. When this happened, the language that sat and rested in every corner of my world, from grocery store signs to traffic-light conversations, began to hide itself from me. The erosion happened gradually—I read road signs without really reading them for years before I realized that I had memorized the shapes of the characters and the streets associated with them rather than what the characters themselves stood for. When my parents spoke to me in a blend of Mandarin, Cantonese, and English, I felt meanings form in my brain without registering the individual words—they could have said the sentence all in one language or all three and I would have felt an understanding in the same way.

When I realized that I had effectively become a receptive linguist in a tongue many assume I am fluent in, I found coping methods to appear much more confident than I really was. I retained my ability to verbally understand Mandarin, and in a pinch, I could hear a sentence in my brain and force it out of my mouth. But whenever I did that, it always felt as if something was missing, or off, and I feared that everyone else noticed as well. This fear drove me to distance myself further from my (m)other tongue until 2019, when I finally decided to relearn the way characters sit inside my mouth—to once again see and be able to read the second language that lives around me.

* * *

In the beginning, classes were tricky for me—I could understand spoken speech and knew I had the ability to speak. However, I had lost the ability to read Mandarin and could not write characters from memory. The gaps in my knowledge were frequent, and the things I had retained were surprising.

Relearning Mandarin feels like walking through a childhood home at twilight—all five of my senses are still intact, and they're all feeding me information, but I can't get the full picture without working for it. All the things that I hear—the tick of a fan, the way a door clicks shut—register cleanly and clearly. But the things that I see are all half-shadows, and they only stir a faint recollection.

Seeing "蔬菜" (shū cài/vegetables) tickles something in me. I know that "艹" is usually used to refer to grasses, fruits, plants, and there's "木" (mù/wood), so that's another sign that points to plants . . . but the rest of it refuses to reveal itself. It isn't until my tutor reads them aloud that the phrase slides smoothly into my brain fully formed.

Through the experience of hearing and seeing the characters in front of me, I feel like I've remembered which switch turns on the lights in the living room.

Once the living room's light is on, the rest comes with surprising ease. I know without having to double check that "南瓜"[16] (nán guā) rather than "冬瓜"[17] (dōng guā) means pumpkin, because assigning "冬瓜" to a pumpkin is as ridiculous as calling a pumpkin a carrot in English just because they're both orange.

In these moments, relearning Mandarin is nothing but pure joy. I read a certain sort of poetry through every character I learn, like how "捉" (zhuō)[18] is composed of 扌and 足, which stand for hand and foot respectively. This makes me giggle as I murmur, "*Because you use your hands and feet to catch!*"

But this is when the doubt settles in; the characters that I relearn and memorize the quickest are the ones that are pictorial, or the ones I can make sense of within the context of English.

Will understanding Mandarin, the language that's technically meant to be my mother tongue, in English actually allow me to relearn how to read and write Mandarin? Is this an authentic connection that I am reforging with my mother tongue?

The need to understand Mandarin in terms of English, a language I have spent my whole life learning and refining, makes my newly rediscovered connection to Mandarin feel cheap—as if there's a sheet of glass standing between me and my childhood home.

Thankfully, it's not a box. There are gaps where I can reach through the invisible barrier I've spent years building to touch my childhood once again. The order in which the strokes of a character should be written still comes to me naturally. Every now and then, I'll recognize a character before it's read aloud. Hearing one phrase makes me think of another. I am playing hide and seek with the elusive version of myself that's fluent in Mandarin.

As of right now, I'm not fluent enough to write analytical essays in Mandarin, but I can speak it again without the fear that something

16 Nán guā: pumpkin
17 Dōng guā: winter melon
18 Zhuō: catch

will feel off. I've rearranged the furniture in my childhood home so that it's accessible again, so that I can become familiar with the old in a new way.

The Tree Next Door

The first time this plumeria tree shows up as a photograph on my phone is January 25, 2016. It's taken from a low angle, and it's hard to make out where the branches end and leaves begin, but it cuts a sharp outline against the sky. It looks like black lace, the insides of a lung, or perhaps a series of clustered peacocks.

After that first photo, hundreds more fill my camera roll.

Some of them are taken on crystal clear days—the light falls just right, and you can see each vein as it splits pinnately from the leaf's midrib. Other times, I'm in a hurry to leave the house, and the tree becomes a blur of bright pinks and mossy greens set on fire by the nearby street lamp.

Despite the fact that the tree belongs to the neighbor—its roots dig itself firmly into a corner of their garden—I come to think of the tree as ours.

When Snapchat finally appears on my radar in late 2016, I realize that I have a means to share the beauty of this tree with a whole new audience. My friends receive photos of the plumeria tree with the sun spinning through its branches or a sliver of the moon peeking through its leaves.

I document it obsessively across early mornings and humid afternoons—in the dead of the night, with only orange lamplight humming across the broad, even leaves. I catch the shadow it casts across our garden wall and the curves of its stems.

Once, I manage to catch it in the rain.

Its newly fallen flowers press their petals into the concrete of our driveway, and I have the sudden urge to decipher what they're trying to say, as if the plumeria tree has learned Morse code just for me.

*   *   *

From August 2017 to April 2019, my camera roll is curiously empty of the plumeria tree. I am abroad, studying at a university in Canada, far from any location tropical enough to sustain the sweetness of nighttime plumeria.

Still, I get to see the tree from home; in my absence, my sisters begin the ritual of documenting the plumeria tree. They send me a snap every morning, just as they're about to leave for school. Even an ocean away and reduced to the size of an iPhone 6 screen, the tree is beautiful.

But only ever seeing it through a screen after years of tangible interaction dulls my reaction to the tree. With each *"good morning, here's the tree"* snap I form an increased apathy towards it. My eyes scan over the tree disinterestedly, wandering across the shape of the leaves and registering no change or movement.

Overexposure to the digital plumeria tree sticks it in a box with Schrödinger's cat. It's certainly not *dead*, but I don't view it as alive anymore.

*   *   *

It is the summer of 2019, and I am home again. My interest has been caught by the *Bucida molineti* trees. To my sheer joy, the *B. molineti* trees (which I've colloquially termed "umbrella trees" due to the circular spread of its branches) have exploded with growth. Once shorter than me, the tops of them can now only be seen from the second floor. For weeks, I photograph the umbrella trees and the way their shadows rotate around them like a clock with one hand.

During my first thunderstorm of the summer, I watch the heavy rain pull leaf after leaf from my trembling umbrellas. In the aftermath, our grass looks as if it's coated with gleaming beetle wings.

Every now and then—when the light is particularly striking or when I notice my sisters taking a photograph of the plumeria tree, I grab a photograph of it too. But mostly my interest is pinned to our newly fruiting papaya tree, the reach of our bougainvillea, the bitter ginger flowers . . .

It isn't until my mother sprints into the house that my attention refocuses. Her hands are moving faster than the Mandarin spilling out of her mouth: *Come take a photograph of it before it disappears! They're cutting it down!*

I malfunction, struggling to figure out what "it" could be. When my mother disappears back out the front door, the plumeria tree blooms—sharp and bright with all its peacocks perched in its branches.

My feet take me outside in the blink of an eye, and my phone is already raised to catch a man up in the branches of the plumeria tree. He's holding a long knife and tapping, patiently, at the places where branch meets trunk.

There are no churning chainsaws or the whine of metal as it bites into wood, but it cuts through me all the same.

For a long bittersweet moment, the plumeria tree is wholly alive. Today, it is half cast in light, half in deep shadow. I mechanically take photos of the tree. *One. Two.*

My mother is not taking photographs, but her fingers are worrying at her phone as she argues with the gardeners. They've been hired by our neighbors to clear and cement up the garden to avoid maintenance costs, and the gardeners insist that the tree is included in their order to clear the garden. And besides, they tell us in Malay: *"It isn't like they want to be cutting the tree down."*

My hands and feet move on their own accord. *Three. Four. Five. Six. A video, for good measure.*

When the phone call finally comes through, a series of worried words cross from owner to gardener, and the knife is put down.

I take another photo—*seven*—and put away my phone.

Tang Yuan

I write this mostly as a reminder to myself, for the future, about the kinds of stories that are bound up in the intricate, time-consuming recipes that you make with people. The writing of this involved me going to my mother and asking her exactly how she makes the soup. I write this as an invitation to you to make tang yuan yourself.

Instructions

- *Gently wash the skin of an orange and purple sweet potato.*[19]

- *Cover them with holes poked with a fork and put them into a pot of cold water.*

- *Boil them until a fork can be poked in and cleanly and easily pulled out.*

- *Cut eleven pandan leaves from a bush and chop it up into pieces small enough for the juicer to handle. Revel in the sweetness of the new cut-plant smell.*

- *Pound the cut and juiced pandan pieces with a mortar and pestle and a little bit of water to get the last of the chlorophyll.*

- *Make green tang yuan by mixing glutinous rice flour with the pandan juice (not too much, however, elsewise there will be a slight bitterness that transfers from the leaf to the dessert).*

---

19 In North American grocery stores, these are typically called "yams" and "Asian yams," respectively.

- *Orange tang yuan are made out of glutinous rice flour and mashed bits of the orange sweet potato, adding plain water as needed.*

- *Make pink tang yuan out of a mixture of food dye and water (unless you have the time to buy and juice a pink dragonfruit).*

- *Purple tang yuan are made when the water a purple sweet potato is boiled in.*

- *White is made last, satisfyingly clean.*

- *Pinch off a bit of the dough and roll it between your palms till it makes a small ball roughly 1 cm in diameter. Form them as evenly as you can, to make estimating cook times easier.*

- *When all of the colorful spheres are made and arrayed in rings and floral patterns around you, cook them in boiling water. You'll know they're cooked when their color grows vivid and they float to the top of the pot.*

- *Cut a second set of pandan leaves close to the stalk, wash each blade thoroughly, layer them on top of each other, and tie the leaves into a knot so that it's easy to fish them out of the soup once it has been cooked.*

- *While the balls of dough are being made, start preparing to make the sugar soup with thick slices of ginger, brown sugar, and the pandan leaf knot.*

- *When serving, make sure to have at least one of each color in the bowl.*

Share with family. Celebrate the winter solstice, and if you have a birthday like mine, be grateful for this opportunity to gather with those close to you to celebrate an early announcement of a trip around the sun.

(M)otherland

"You are distance."

Time is loosening in my hands
like liquid rubber
pooling at my feet.

I am listening to the car hum over road,
feeling us move without feeling the curve of the earth—
instead there is the hush
of the tires as they grip, pick up, and release stormwater.

It seems that for every tree I learn,
Malaysia plants another—
one with pink flowers (all stamens)
but on a tree as large and as pinnated with its leaves
like the flame of the forest.

I am trying to learn my mother(land)
through her plants
in the same way as I have learned my other land
by identifying flowering bushes and big-leafed trees.

I am doing this
as if knowing another rendition of her geography
will map me onto this place
the way it has mapped onto me.

Originally written July 2019

Chinese New Year

My homes dissolve in a flurry of preparations:
every year it is the same—
red lanterns appear magically, hung and artfully arranged
as artificial blooms in the trees around our house,
a red diamond with "福"[20] written onto it flowers across our doors
    upside down.
We are filling our lives with good fortune for the new year.

And every year, we run through this—these rituals.
We tell the stories of monsters and good luck.
We welcome the lion dancers with heads of lettuce and mandarins
and surreptitiously pause our brooms until just the right day
while filling the sky with colored sparks at night.

We light candles and watch the wax melt into a light green waterfall
as our fingers pick up the smell of smoke
from throwing tiny packets of exploding powder at the ground.

At my uncles' houses, we set off long strings of firecrackers
with fingers plugged into our ears.
Our bodies are sticky and hot and trapped in our fancy clothes.
Our chopsticks clatter as we sift through the *yee sang*,[21]
raising it high and raining down bits of pomelo and mango,
pickled ginger, smoked salmon, sesame seeds, and crunchy
    fried dough.

....

20   Fú: a character that signifies blessings and good fortune
21   a Cantonese-style dish designed to amplify and encourage prosperity for all
    who partake in the tossing of the ingredients (the higher you toss, the more
    prosperity there is; also known as *lo hei* or *yuu sahng*)

We gather for photographs, arranging ourselves by family,
by height and generation,
by gender and ancestry—
we smile until our cheeks hurt and then we smile some more,
knowing that this is the one occasion in which we come together.

We eat our grandparents' favorite dishes:
there are *ang ku kuehs*[22] and *nasi minyak,*[23]
there is *nasi dagang*[24] and pineapple tarts,
crab and sweet and sour fish.

As kids we run around with eager hands,
mouths tripping over the familiar 新年快乐[25] so that we can receive
the highly anticipated 红包.[26]
Our relatives give us prosperity and words of advice,
and we wish them a 身体健康[27] in return.

We gather at altars and sift prayer beads between our fingers.
My mouth is filled with vowel after vowel.
Itching down my back is the guilt of incomprehension.
I sigh heavy, trying to cool myself with the exhale of warm breath,
and the fan blows it right back into my face
as rising incense tickles my nose.

....

22 a bite-sized snack food of an orange glutinous rice flour skin wrapped around a
    sweet mung bean filling (known in English as "red tortoise cake")—it is one of
    my grandmother's favorite dishes
23 a version of a fragrant rice dish where the rice is yellow, pink, and red and is
    commonly eaten with a spicy chicken rendang (literally translated as "oil rice")
24 a version of a fragrant rice dish that is eaten with a fish curry and pickled
    cucumber and carrots called *achar* (literally translated as "fish rice")
25 Xìng nián kuài lè: Happy New Year
26 Hóng bāo: red envelope
27 Shēn tǐ jiàn kāng: healthy body

A lot of the magic reveals itself to me as I get older—
everything reveals its story, and perhaps, for the first time, I am
    ready to listen.
I learn that it is not the work of fairies but rather my elders.
And then it becomes me, helping to hang the decorations,
me who cleans the smooth stretch of marble floor,
who fills and carries out the dishes that weigh down table after table.

A lot of the magic reveals that it has been hiding in the dedicated act
of keeping rituals alive—
and in my house, my mother spearheads it all.
In the span of four days, dozens of cartons of oranges appear
as if there's a secret orchard in my backyard I never knew about.
Container after container of *nga ku*[28] chips and *kek lapis*[29] start
    amassing on a cupboard,
label side pointed out as if they are preparing for a contest.

My mom drives far and wide to track them down:
the *kuih bangkit*,[30] the love letters, the 年糕.[31]
My sisters and I spend hours peeling plastic strips off delicately
    cut shapes
to reveal double-sided tape that holds together red lanterns,
and yellow or orange pineapples.
We hang them up amongst the branches of the plumeria tree
and hide them in my mom's jasmine bushes.

....

28 arrowroot
29 literally translates to "layer cake"
30 small coconut cream cookies that melt in your mouth
31 Nián gāo: year cake

We soak pre-cut long beans in buckets of water
before we stir fry them with pickled radish.
Cans of sugared liquid get submerged in ice.
Pots of orchids exhale open in all corners of my house.

We reign in the dogs as sweat trickles down our backs,
and family trickles in through the gates in irregular intervals.
At once, we get a flood of people and all of a sudden the kitchen
is thrown into high gear.
We steam noodles for *chee cheong fun*[32] and chop cucumbers as fast
  as we can.

The kitchen fills with heat and steam—
it roils around us until my glasses feel permanently fogged.
Over and over, I learn that Chinese New Year is a time
of food and love and connection.
I learn the stories behind my great aunt's black vinegar soup
and the rhyme and reason behind each day of the new year.

Over and over, the lunar new year reminds me
to share when I have little
and be grateful for what I receive in return.
Over and over, I learn to say:
谢谢大家.[33]

---

32 a Cantonese steamed rice noodle roll dish
33 Xiè xiè dà jiā: Thank you, everyone

CANADA

Acknowledgement

Am I allowed?
This is a tentative question, a hesitant, quiet ask.
English lends itself poetically to our understanding of space—
We have a "sense of place" that is known, and felt, and kept
because to know a place is somehow always better than
   knowing nowhere.
We can tell people to "know their place" and call others
   "marginalized" . . .

And so the question arises:
Am I allowed to belong here?
Here, I am marginalized—I am the space that exists between the
   edge of the page
and all of the words, and voices, and narratives of those whose
   stories are centered here.
I don't know what that means yet—or how to be that space
when I'm not sure how
to take up space—
I am so used to holding space for others.

I don't know how to be blank such that I can be filled with that
   which is here
because it already feels as if I am spilling across boundaries
   and borders—
because it always feels like I am crossing lines on a map.
But there is no space I can find,
no X that marks the spot,
no shape that I can find that fits me.

I can find no place for me to put down the fact that today, and
    every day,
I hold the weight of entire countries on my shoulders.
But I am reading the words around me
and learning the stories of the Serpent and the Cedar
so that I can learn this new land of mine.

And I appreciate the weight of countries—
they remind me that I have a sense of places.

Tongue

Feet planted, hands spread wide—
there is something that's been bugging me, nagging me
like sounds that look like they should go together but don't.

Like ... ketchup *and* tomatoes on a grilled cheese sandwich.

My feet are planted in three worlds, and I know that makes no sense
because I only have two feet ...
But my feet are planted, and I am here to inform you with my
    hands wide
(wide like your eyes should be, wide like your ears should be,
wide like the mouth of the wolf from *Little Red Riding Hood*).
I am here to inform you that I speak English because Malaysia
    (yes, Asia)
was colonized by the British, the Portuguese, and the Dutch.
The British, the language of *u's* in your favo[u]rite colo[u]rs,
yet, unlike Mandarin and Spanish,
which have 你和您[34] and *tú y usted*[35]—
the British just have "you."
You who are questioning, eyes seeking like roving horses running
    across plains.
You who are wondering: *How? Why?*
You who are impressed, and the astonishment annoys me—

34 Nǐ hé nín: you (informal) and you (formal) in Mandarin
35 you (informal) and you (formal) in Spanish

I speak English because I grew up in international schools with
    letters lining the walls,
with alphabet soup and Cheerio *o*'s, and the notion of marking maps
with an *x, y,* and *z*.

Growing up I had picture books:
Here's the cow (it goes moo); here is a yacht (it's not really
    intuitively spelt, spelled).
Here is a line, a queue, not the letter but the noun, the verb, the
    faint impression
of more elegant things, like the queens that gaze from colored bits
    of paper—
postage stamps and money.

Your stare can't send me back to where I came from
because it's here, there, everywhere.

I grew up with two languages on my tongue
(like the way it feels when you have two scoops of ice cream, and in
    one go, you get a bit
of both—vanilla *and* green tea).
There are strokes I could paint in the air with broad sweeps and
    strokes that mean "star."
It is a word composed of a sun and a birth,
a word that sounds like the word for heart.

So here I stand, feet planted, hands wide,
defiant and proud of the strings that have tied around my heart,
    my star,
around my mouth that's open like the first spring bloom.
It's an anticipatory wait—*Oh! The words I get to curate.*

I think the better question is: Why shouldn't I have more than one
  hat or more than one shoe?—
A pair is, after all, normal.

There is a part of me that knows (nose) that it's suitable to
  be astonished
when this language called English has three words for two, to,
  and too.
But I raise you one, with a Mandarin poem composed entirely
  of *shi's*.[36]
Impress me.

....

36 施氏食獅史 (shī-shì shí shī shǐ): the "Lion-Eating Poet in the Stone Den" is a
    classic tongue-twister poem.

Autumn

The fireworks explode and I think immediately
of Malaysia and its new years—
the ones based on slightly different versions
of the lunar calendar: Chinese New Year, Ramadan, Diwali—

As the sky turns into a series of whistles and colored smoke
I ask the people around me: "*Is this normal . . .?*"
We twist in time to music and cold air
and I repeat my question: " *. . . the fireworks?*"

They shrug noncommittally.
"*Maybe it's a Squamish thing.*"
"*A Squamish thing,*" I echo.
Squamish things, like how to wear layers and find warmth,
where to buy ginger to slice and put into hot water;
the magical things, like the first snowfall and the changing golds
   of maples;
and the harder things, like walks in the woods where I feel
like a stranger in a strange country.

There is another smattering of lights in the sky, and I
   turn, mesmerized—
seeking out the bits of bright in the darkest dark.
The crowd around me sinks themselves
into bottles of strong-smelling liquid, celebrating the occasion.

It is Halloween, and this means that there are bowls of candy,
and houses wrapped in cobwebs and dotted with skeletons.
It is Halloween, and I guess it means
that there are fireworks in the sky.

"Fireworks on Halloween," I murmur.
It is hard to tell if anyone around me is as enthralled as I am.

I leave the seething mass of heat and color—
I go into my room and turn off the lights.
And for a while, I stand in the dark and watch sparks shatter
    through the sky.
For a while, with the heater running and the sound of thunder in
    the air,
I can pretend that I am home.

Uprooting

My mother is hurt when the word slips quickly and easily from
    my mouth—
in one breath, I have changed the land of mountains and cold from
    an alien, unreachable thing
into a place near enough to pull into the chambers of my
    warm heart—
I call it home and shoot an arrow
clean through her.

I feel as if I have betrayed
some sort of inherent root within me.

Like I've reached into my mother's chest
and uprooted
myself—
less a disentangling
and more the yank
of tender tap root from soil.

I feel like
a parasitic orchid whose home happens to be wherever it can latch
    on and grow.
To think of the dark, the rain, the clean white snow—

To think . . .
she calls it *home*.

Mooncake Festival

A friend remarks to me after googling the mooncake: *"Did you know that it has 950 kcal?"*

I am startled out of my reverie, my recollection of some of my fondest childhood memories. Because I am slow to respond, slow to defend, my friend rolls onwards: *"No way! Why would you eat something like this!"*

There is an embarrassed warmth in my chest. I blush and stammer, saying that I hadn't been aware of how awful the mooncake is for your health.

A couple of weeks later, when the mooncakes arrive, packaged neatly in a red-colored box covered with blooming peonies, the fear of being shamed for wanting to share something so fatty prompts me to secret the mooncakes away and eat them alone. I gorge myself on the sweet denseness of the lotus-paste filling, crumbling the salty egg yolk in half, as if to share, and then eating the whole thing—like a monster swallowing the sun.

It is 2017, and it is my first Mooncake Festival away from my family.

* * *

Years later, in a phone call with my friend Zoe, this story tumbles out quickly—a confession. She murmurs her regret, and shares with me that the story of *Chang E* is one that sits very close to her heart. We delight in all that we have learned to share—the smallest of mooncakes cut into as many slices as there are people. Our tongues dive through the flavors—lotus paste, red bean, black sesame, the one filled with shavings of nuts that, to this day, remains our least favorite.

Every year, we agree, the Mooncake Festival teaches us that we are lucky and loved by being a time in which family and friends gather together to share. We share descriptions of the salty sweetness, of the unadulterated joy of cutting into a mooncake that has a yolk at its dead center. I tell Zoe about the mooncakes that have arrived this year in the form of photos in my family group chats. There are *agar agar* mooncakes with suspended flowers and dates, *bing pi*[37] mooncakes, and the traditional golden ones, with their glistening egg wash. She makes sounds of delight, and we allow a brief pause for the wave of mournfulness that comes with not being able to celebrate this year.

To make up for this fact—our lack of mooncakes, our lack of togetherness—we decide to collapse generations and cross the Pacific together, traveling to a time and place of great love for the light of the moon by telling the story of *Chang E*.

"*There are so many versions of this story,*" she tells me on the phone as the sky dims through twilight for the both of us in the Pacific Northwest. "*But this is the one I have been told growing up, that I am so honored to share with you.*"

* * *

"*There was once a beautiful young woman named Chang E, who existed in the Jade Palace. She was fair-skinned, and had long dark hair like the night, and red lips like plums. One night, she had the misfortune of breaking a vase that was very precious to the Jade Emperor. He banished her and sent her away to live on earth with a family of farmers. As she grew, she befriended a man in the village named Hou Yi.*

"*One day, Hou Yi shots down nine of the ten suns—which is a story of its own, but it doesn't get told today because this is a story of the moon.*

"*There was a huge celebration, and Hou Yi married Chang E. They lived in the palace as king and wife, but over the years, power started to go to Hou Yi's head—he rejected the way of life taught to him in childhood and became mean and selfish.*

37 冰皮 (bīng pí; snow skin): Snow skin mooncakes are a new type of mooncake that don't need to be baked.

"*Chang E tried to bring him back, but nothing she said or did could do so. That was when she remembered that on the fateful day in which Hou Yi shot down the nine suns, he was gifted with the elixir of life. With the power of immortality, the elixir only had enough to serve one human. It was Hou Yi's most prized possession.*

"*In that moment, Chang E knew that she had to take the elixir so that Hou Yi wouldn't be able to continue his tyrannical life. She snuck into his room, stole the elixir, went out onto the roof, and drank it.*

"*When Hou Yi learned that the elixir was gone, he frantically searched the palace, ending up on the roof. But he was too late, for Chang E was already ascending into the heavens. He pulled an arrow out of his quiver and tried to shoot her down, but every arrow missed. He watched her rise up and up.*

"*Chang E was sent to the moon—and stories vary—but when she ascended into the heavens, I have been told that she was greeted by a bridge illuminated by moonlight. As a reward of her act—one full of altruism and a deep care for the people of the kingdom—Chang E was granted the title of 'Goddess of the Moon,' and there she still lives.*

"*She went on to watch her husband grow old down on earth. She watched him transform as he mourned her into a king that no longer hurts his people. When he died, after becoming a fair and just ruler, the gods granted him one last gift by having him ascend onto the last of the suns. Together, Hou Yi and Chang E become yin and yang. On full moons, Hou Yi admires Chang E's beauty. They will see each other from a distance for the rest of time while watching their human connections on earth grow old and pass away. Now, they continue to watch over us.*"

Stillness

I lie flat on the ground and listen to my heart
beat
right through my fingertips.

Today we learned about neutrinos,
which pass right through us all day long without knowing
that we exist.

I wonder what I pass by—through—without notice,
without being noticed.

I take a seven-minute shower in the dark.
Think only
of the feel of water running over skin.

Blackberries

I want to go playground hunting with someone;
smear our faces with road-side blackberries and wrap purple fingers
around faded-yellow metal poles.
We would dive out of truck beds, tucking and rolling onto streets
    named after trees—
Chestnut, Cottonwood, Pine—
at the merest glimpse of a well-loved slide.

When I was younger, there was an overgrown playground
that we—my father, my sisters, and I—would go to.
We would walk over heated roads, past rusted metal gates, and up a
    tunnel of trees.
The slide was as pink as our cheeks, and the touch-me-nots
would shiver closed as they brushed our chests.

Here I ride the bus
and watch those familiar
with the geography of these neighborhoods take to the streets
through a window fogged by mist or summer rain.

When I was younger the three of us would take turns swinging,
a creaking symphony of chain and seat as our father caught us,
pushed us away,
and trusted the forces of the world to bring us back to him—

Slightly stronger,
slightly braver.

The Mountains, Part One

An honest truth:

The mountains inspired a sense of awe and wonder in me the day I first saw them, driving up to the little gray-blue building next to Tim Horton's in a Greyhound Bus that no longer runs. It was August 30, 2017. I was jet-lagged and too overwhelmed by all the new things to begin experiencing homesickness.

The mountains were a series of sharp ridges—unbroken by the mirrors of skyscrapers or a breathing, vibrating mass of electrical wiring. Instead, they broke the sky.

Looking at them, I felt a little quieter. Somehow, their solid granite faces made me coalesce firmly into myself.

An honest fear:

They stood tall over me the day I first saw them. There and then began the silent, unsettling feeling that I might not belong here.

My feet grew up learning how to walk amongst flat, massive sprawls of cities and sandy coastlines. My eyes were fond of watching the sun rise and set over a series of houses, the horizon cracking the sun in half like a fork piercing a yolk and spilling it across the sky.

Here, the mountains spit and swallow the sun at times that run counter to my intuitive clock. It is as if, for the mountains, a star is as easy to stomach and digest as the golden flesh of a mango.

An honest moment:

I swim from one side of a lake to the other and back for the first time.

I watch paddle boarders out of the corner of my eyes and make water angels.

I learn that swimming in a straight line is about as futile as trying to keep a handful of dry sand from escaping your grasp.

I've seen the open stretch of sky from the top of the second largest granite monolith in the world twice now—once in time for noontime sun with people who believed in me, and once in time for a summer solstice sunrise.

I haven't stood atop the spines of the sleeping giants around me, but it is comforting to know that I might one day—that I will one day.

ABC Soup

I call my mother to ask how she makes it, but I am ahead of
    my time—
she is asleep twelve thousand, seven hundred, and thirty-four
    kilometers away.
But the pot is already on the stove, and there are people waiting,
so I turn to the internet.
The recipe calls for *zhà cài*[38] and pork ribs, and I have neither—
but I have almost everything else:
the onions, potatoes, tomatoes, carrots, ginger, garlic, water, salt,
    and pepper.

The cutting is familiar, at least. Chopping off the top and the
    bottom of the onion,
halving it and peeling off the dry layers before cutting them
    into chunks.
Aloud, I say: "*This is what we do*
when I am at home—I cut, and my mother cooks."
I chop the potatoes into inch-thick bricks, the tomatoes into
    wedges, carrots into rounds.
The garlic is diced and the ginger sliced,
and then everything goes into the pot with a generous helping
    of water.

I watch the water simmer and come to a roiling boil.
Together, the onions and the tomatoes sweeten the steam.
My glasses fog up as I inhale the salted warmth and poke at the
    slowly cooking potatoes.

....
38   榨菜 (*zhà cài*): pickled mustard green

By the time the soup is ready, my mother has called me back, asking
    if anything is wrong.
"Nothing's wrong," I say, *"I just wanted to make soup."*
I talk her through my process, lamenting the lack of *zhà cài*,
and my worry that it'll taste wrong.
"Don't worry," she assures, *"ABC soup is called ABC soup
because it's as easy as A-B-C. And it always tastes like home."*

BHUTAN

First Impressions

I am standing in a hallway with only the buzzing of nighttime cicadas and the whir of bugs being pulled to the light to accompany me; it is the only place in my dorm building where my phone connects to the internet. The hallways are open to the air, with the railings facing the mountains across the valley.

I thought about my phone approximately four times today, and each thought began with: *I should take a photo of this to share with my family.*

Bhutan has so far been the most comforting, most disquieting blend of the East and the West, in that the culture and the colors and the food remind me of my Asian self. But the climate and flora remind me of my Western self, the one that knows how to identify the things that surround her. Both are caught in the meeting of new people, with my voice belying my face: *"Hi, my name is Yin Xzi."*

The East explodes in the form of a vegetable market that sprawls through the underside of a building and the leaning of willow trees. It shows up in hot cups of milk tea and the practice of handwashing clothes.

But the West creeps in in the form of buttercups and street-side roses, sunflowers, and hydrangea bushes. It shows up in the pine trees outside my window and in the university's library where I find a copy of Robin Wall Kimmerer's *Braiding Sweetgrass.*

The mountain ridges are a combination of the round evergreens of Malaysia and the sharp cuts of Canada. Today, I spent the car ride up from Thimphu Valley to where the campus is located in Ngabiphu, poring over my *Butterflies of Bhutan* book with a fellow exchange student and new friend, Oscar. We talk about the butterflies that overlap between here, my homes, and his. Mostly, I learn that we name many butterflies after birds and colors, like the one named "pale grass blue."

*　*　*

Here, my assumed identity, until I open my mouth and ruin the image, is that I am Bhutanese. Strangers greet me in a flurry of Dzongkha that I can make no sense of; it is all just sounds. How strange and refreshing it is to have it immediately assumed that I belong here. How utterly, bone-shakingly weird.

I wore a *kira* for the first time today to see what size I should buy. The shopkeeper sized me up with a single look and nailed it.

Temple

What an image we make:
a series of brown and tan bodies rising and falling in unison,
locked together in prayer.
We press our foreheads into polished wood or the cool rough
 of stone.

I wonder what it must be like to walk into your place of quiet faith,
place your forehead on the floor,
and know that you are being watched by light-colored eyes
 and echoed
by the distinct crack of a camera shutter falling closed.

Strange, how temples and monasteries hold a sense of childhood,
the stretching stillness of the lotus pose and the sifting of
 prayer beads.
Stranger still, it turns out that I know people here—
graduates of the school, aunts and uncles of my classmates.

I say that I am from Malaysia,
like the Hup Seng Cream Crackers they are fond of dipping in their
 milk tea.
"The biscuits?" they exclaim. I smile and nod,
and we are joyous in this new connection—the crackers, them,
 and I.

Wrapped around my waist is a purple sarong, one brought
 from home.
Falling from my mouth are the words for hello and thank you:
Kuzu zangpo la, gadrinche.

Kira

It is one of the first rites I learn, second only to how to eat
rice (and spice and dhal) at every meal.
My roommates fuss over me, as though I am their little sister.

First is the *kira*—the skirt. I have a ready-made half *kira*.
It comes complete with Velcro and a clip for easy fastening,
designed in part for young children and also for the ease of *chillips*.[39]
In this moment, I am both.

Kristina shows me how to hold the half kira up to my waist,
with the fold falling to the side of my right thigh as Yeshey wraps
her arms around me, pinning the Velcro to itself at my left waist,
and then bringing the rest of the fabric around my back to clip on
    my right.
They nod, adjusting the cloth so that the bottoms of the skirt
    hang even.

Then comes the *wonju*—the inner shirt.
Mine is a light maroon, and they both smile in approval of the color.
The bottom hem of it ends just below my waist,
but its sleeves trail a whole hand's length off my arms.
I then pull on the *toego*—the outer shirt, a color deeper than the
    blue of the sky.
Kristina fidgets with my collar as Yeshey adjusts the shirtsleeves.
The *wonju* is tucked over the *toego*, whose collar is then flipped.
Kristina reaches her arm up my shirts in order to pin the
    layers together.
A second one is fastened near the bottom.

....

39   a phrase in Bhutan used to refer to a foreigner

They show me how to shake my arms out to fold the longer sleeve
of the *wonju* up over the *toego*,
then how to grip the slippery insides of the *wonju* in order to roll
    my sleeves
up and over themselves one more time.

As I walk through the school during the day,
I learn that I have far more older sisters than I have ever imagined.
My classmates teach me how to wrap my *kera*—the belt—once I
    graduate to wearing my full *kira*,
which is a large beautiful piece of cloth that is belted at the waist
and fastened at the shoulders by a pair of clips known as the *koma*.

When I wear my *kira*, I become a part of the school—
less another *chillip* and more *here*.
Sither fixes my hems, and I compliment the colors of her *toego*;
Tshokey fixes my sleeves and my forever unrolling collar whenever I
    walk by.

Here, For You

I take a photo, and immediately
we are thousands of kilometers away,
traveling in a bubble on my phone.

I take a video, and already
you know what the mountains sound like—
the waterfalling hums of crickets,
the rush of wind through bamboo—
I haven't even processed it,
and already my phone delivers it to you.

But it is missing things,
and so you miss me—
you miss the way our stomachs curdle
and what my dreams are,
and so instead of this—
this photo, this video, I give you this . . .

Last night, the main street of Thimphu was blocked
for the visit of India's prime minister.
After he left, people spilled into the streets,
wandering through the cooling evening air.
There were kids with plastic soccer balls
and monks walking in pairs.
They ate ice cream out of cups with a popsicle stick.

We catch rides for free more often than not—
a thumb stuck out into the air—
hotter and drier than I would have anticipated for two o'clock

in the afternoon during monsoon season.
Cars roll to a slow stop and we shout out our destination:
    "Clock Tower?"
"Ok," comes the reply, with a head nudge that we've quickly gotten
    used to.
We pull open the car doors and pile inside,
like heavy bags of sand
with our settling road dust.

We stumble up into the forest with the campus dogs.
Slowly we learn their names.
Handsome.
Sunny.
Chip, Biggy, Tenzin, Shaggy.
Maggie.

We get caught in sudden heavy rainfall.
It pours off of roofs and turns the hill into a slip and slide.
The front of my *kira* is soaked, and my rain jacket is one meter away
from being just a wet piece of cloth on my body.
My roommate's friend Pema offers me shelter
under her umbrella, and we shrink and sprint
down to the academic building,
laughing as we spill,
sopping wet and dripping water in the lobby.

We climb up three hundred and eighty-eight steps,
and my breath is taken away by the intricate carvings
that wind up the columns of the Buddha Dordenma.
My fingers itch to take a photo, but the signs around me remind me
    not to.
Instead of photographing, I kneel.
Touch my head to the ground.

I select postcards from the gift shops
and fill their empty backs with cramped small handwriting.
With two stamps, the postcards leave me
and take weeks to arrive.

For my pen pals, the experiences are unfolding as they read them,
though I have already moved on to new adventures.

The Mountains, Part Two

Sometime before sunset, the eight of us set up camp for the night—
two blue four-person tents and Lacey's orange two-person one.
Alaina wanders amongst the purple *halenia elliptica*,
the pink-tipped thistles, and tiny bunches of yellow aster flowers.
Earlier, Alaina had put peanut butter on an almond
and dipped it in honey, and after our long hike,
the combination tastes like ambrosia.

We started the day by being awoken
by a horse outside our tent, curiously nosing through our rain fly
at the three kilograms of oranges, and two of plums, and one of
apples that we'd brought along.
Ben and Brendan stepped out into the morning dew, stretching.

In the light of the morning, the backyard of the house we were
allowed to camp in
seemed to extend for ages, clear across the valley and up into
the mountains.
We have rice and *kewa datzi*[40] for breakfast.
Our cook and sudden new friend, Karma, guides us to the trout
farm across the river and down the road.
Oscar pets a sturgeon, and Tori gives me a flower, which I
gladly return.

Today, I saw autumn in the making:
the flurry of activity in the leaves as they charge through my sisters'
earliest favorite colors.

---

40   a potato (kewa) dish cooked in cheese (datzi), common throughout the country

The canopy cover was thinner today than it was when we
    first arrived—
the floor a little softer from all the fallen needles.
It is a rearrangement of geography—
paths that were once creek beds are suddenly exposed rock, slick
    with moss.

Now, Lacey and Tori walk barefoot—
one collects firewood; the other accidentally steps into a cow patty.
Rachel puts her camera on a log and waits
for the fire to be started as we trickle in from the hills
and gather for a family photo.

We laugh as the camera shutter clicks open and shut seven times.
Stars smear across the night sky, one of them moves; we make
    a wish.

Thimphu

It's monsoon season, the sky reminds us.
The rain drums on the blue roofs of the school and runs down the
    hill with us.
It's monsoon season and it's raining, the clouds whisper as we take
    the bus.
We wind downwards from Ngabiphu through Babesa,
    Olakha, Semtoka,
till Thimphu, where buildings under construction are latticed
    with bamboo
and walls are covered with paintings of the eight auspicious symbols.

At the open air market, Phub Doji pushes a guava into my hands.
He is happy that we have come to visit yet again, his favorite *chillips*
    from the college.
"Sweet, in season, local, lekshom!"[41] he insists, pulling more fruit from
    his selection.
I blush and accept the guava, if only so I am able to gently dissuade
    him from feeding us his entire stall.
I take a bite and am surprised by the sunset inside—
this guava is pink within its yellow. *"Sweet,"* I echo, *"Lekshom."*
His smile splits wide, hands already in motion, weighing out a
    kilogram of the fruit.
"Lekshom!"

The evening air rushes in through the open bus window;
the air smells like simmering onions.
We pass taxis filled with strangers sharing a fare—

41 Good

it's 45 Nu[42] from Clock Tower to Zeropoint,
and the familiarity of the knowledge surprises me.

My head swims through sea after sea of cosmos flowers.
The monks tell us that they appear after rainy season—
a fact that our many months in Bhutan have since refuted—
but it's a quietly endearing image:
flowers that wait until the last drop hits earth
before unfurling their petals and pointing towards light.

Fields of them sway as we walk, as we drive, as we cling
to the sides of roads and step gingerly across stones to avoid
    deep puddles.
Roadsides are surrounded by oceans of cosmos flowers
that interrupt stretch after stretch of rice fields.
The petals undulate in the wind—
waves of white dance along pink and deep purple.

---

42   Nu or *ngultrum* is the currency of Bhutan.

Karaoke

The concept isn't unfamiliar—there is a mic, a big screen,
a bass line reverberating through the air . . .
but there's still a degree of strangeness
in knowing that we have come to this beautiful place
to go to karaoke bars late at night and sing.
Hesitantly, we run our fingers down the list of song options,
reading over familiar English artists.
"This one?" Our heads pull closer together in the dim room to
    appraise the choice.
As we hem and haw, the room fills with the sounds of Dzongkha
    songs crooned by locals.
In the dark, lit only by the screens, we become luminous beings,
united by singing the same words to a beat,
by the faint smell of *ara*[43] and Druk lager in the air.

To the delight of the Bhutanese people in the karaoke place,
we have added a few Dzongkha songs to our repertoire—
the whole room launches into ecstatic cheers when we get up
    on stage.
It is an iconic rendition of "Oh My Sweetheart."[44]
In this, we know Bhutan better than most tourists ever will,
for we know where all of the little stores are hidden, in alleyways
    and up back staircases,
we know that "Old Town Road" is a guaranteed hit
    when performed,
regardless of the age range present.

43 the traditional alcoholic beverage made from barley, rice, or wheat, commonly
    served with egg
44 If you would like to listen to this, look up "Bhutanese Songs, Ho My
    Sweet Heart"

We sing karaoke into the dead of night
and wind a slow, unsteady route back up the hill.
The taxis cough and strain with the effort
of changing gears while on a steep slope,
and we laugh because we understand.

Paro

The fruit and vegetable market in Paro is filled with a blue glow and the faint smell of dried fish, discarded cauliflower bottoms, and the turned earth scent of potatoes and ginger and onions. In the light cast by tarps, the chilis take on the sheen of neon lights—a surreal fold of red and green, of blue and violet.

Amidst the chatter, the sentences I recognize float to the surface: *"Ani gong gademchi mo?"*[45]

For the most part, the numbers come back in English: *"Twenty nu. One hundred for one kilogram."* I watch grandmothers chew *doma*[46] as they hold light purple radishes up to their ears and thrum their fingers across its cool surface. In response, the radish sings the sweet song of rain hitting wet earth.

A mother carries her child wrapped in a scarf across her back as she stoops to sift through a basket of garlic—their dry, papery outsides rustle against her palms.

There's a man in a worn checkered *gho*,[47] who tucks a couple of tomatoes into his pocket. He bids a goodbye to the seller, who nods and reaches up, adjusting the line of drying eggplant slices hanging from a string above her head.

There is a magic in the air that we can't help but be silent spectators of. After having lived in Bhutan for two months, we are less *chillip* than most, but there is still an undercurrent of familiarity among the faces around us that I long to be fluent in.

We weave in and out of the stalls, feet learning the uneven floors as we munch on pomegranate arils and apples larger than my fist.

---

45 "How much is this?"
46 a popular pastime is chewing *doma*, a combination of betel nut, leaf, and lime
47 traditional Bhutanese dress for men

Laya

The bus turns a corner of the winding valley road and the
 mountains appear.
From far below and framed by the window, they look like a series of
 sharp teeth.
Out here, up north, there are only two geographical markers known
 to me: the names Gasa and Laya.

A series of bolero trucks take us along the mountains from Gasa to
 where the hike up to Laya begins.
I am filled with a giddy sort of nervousness, for today I test myself
and my ability to be among the mountains.
Our bags are tied to a fleet of horses that are encouraged up the
 mountain by sharp shouts.
The bells on the horses sing as they step beside us along the wide, flat
 bank of the Mo Chhu.[48]
Slowly, the trail grows steeper, the air progressively colder.
I wiggle my toes inside my hiking boots, wondering at the porters,
who hike beside us in flip flops and wide smiles—teeth colored red
 by *doma*.
As they walk, they laugh and jostle each other and their horses in
 never-ending conversation.
I keep my mouth shut and focus on breathing as we climb through
 thickets of green into gold
and then through a cloud layer until the ragged edges of
 mountainsides across the valley
are covered not with trees but the white of snow.

---

48 "river" in Dzongkha

At the homestay, we are fed rice with radish *datzi*[49]—
it is so out of the ordinary that I find myself lacking the word
   for "radish."
"Radish gadebe lab wong?"[50] I ask the mother of the family.
She takes a second to process that I am a *chillip* and not Bhutanese
   before smiling and answering:
"Your Dzongkha is very good! Radish is *laphu.*"
"Gadrinche," I say in thanks. *"Nga Dzongkha lhap-doh."*[51]
She smiles wider, and the next day, when I am putting on my
   full *kira,*
she rushes over to help me get the folds just right
so my hems hang even over the thermals I'm wearing underneath.
Stepping back, she appraises me and nods her head in approval.
"Jarem tomei."[52]
I blush and adjust my borrowed *rachu*[53] on my left shoulder
before pulling on my jackets, scarves, and beanie.
The combination of extra warm layers ends up hiding most of
   my *kira,*
but the Himalayan mountain air insists I wrap up.

The festival is conducted in a mixture of Dzongkha and the
   local dialect,
so I understand very little of what is being said, but still, I learn—
I learn about how the people of the town of Laya work
   grueling hours,
crawling on their bellies along the ground to collect cordyceps.

---

49 cheese
50 "How do you say radish?"
51 "I'm learning Dzongkha."
52 "You look beautiful."
53 a part of the *kira* worn during formal occasions such as festivals or visit-
     ing temples

I learn that the family we're staying with could buy a helicopter if
    they wanted.
We sit cross-legged on the ground to be served lunch.
It is warm rice and a curry, cooked strips of fatty pork, and an
    ema datzi.[54]
We eat it all with our right hands, and it fills me with a
    deep warmth.
We take meandering tours of the festival's events,
snacking on *momos*[55] filled with cheese and cabbage.
To everyone's delight, Alaina and Oscar win the three-legged race,
and we become swept up in the festivities.
On the hike down, we collect plastic bottles and bags,
filling the large garbage bags we brought as covers for our
    own luggage.
We take off our shoes and socks to cross a frigid river.
I am cold and tired but alive
and filled with the knowledge
that I have been among the mountains here.

---

54   a dish of chilis (*ema*) cooked in cheese (*datzi*)
55   dumplings

Punakha

We wander through a slightly dusty Khuruthang, with only food on
    our minds.
I catch sight of the play of sun on curtained windows,
on the rise–fall chests of sleeping dogs.
The only open restaurant we end up finding is tiny and on the
    second floor of a building.
Its back windows look out onto a balcony packed with plants
and the darting quiver-shadows of sparrows.
We get egg curry and *shamu datzi*,[56] *bathtup* and egg *koka*.[57]
A group of elementary school boys pour in,
singing a song whose refrain sneaks in and out of our ears
    and mouths
for the next three days: *"Ahtz za za za zaiiiiii . . ."*[58]
The owner hands us a bowl of tangerines, and our little warm, sunlit
    world smells
just a touch like Chinese New Year.

Punahka's *dzong*,[59] the Pungthan Dechen Phodrang Dzong, sits
    right near where
the Pho Chhu and Mo Chhu[60] of Punakha's Puna Tsang Chhu
    valley meet.
The fortress itself is a collection of burgundy rubber trees
and bougainvillea vines draped over orchid trees.

....

56 a dish of mushrooms (*shamu*) cooked in cheese (*datzi*)
57 *Bathtup* is a noodle dish popular in certain provinces, while *koka* is a form of
    instant noodles found in most of the country.
58 If you would like to listen to this, look up "Nga Ghi Lab Mi Kha Lu—Crowners"
59 a fortress monastery in Bhutan
60 The Pho and Mo Chhu (also known as the male and female rivers, respectively)
    are the two rivers of Punakha valley.

I spend a while watching the dance of bodhi leaves
and the slip of water over the backs of a school of fish.
The bubbling chatter of tourists and their guides rock in little eddies
        around our quiet heads.
We listen to the guides talk about Guru Rinpoche and Zhabdrung.
After a while, we wander-walk over to the suspension bridge,
laughing at our bottle cap necklaces and the thought of falling
        eucalyptus branches.
We cross the bridge once under the light of the setting sun,
a second in the bending light of the moon.
The valley is warm and filled with the smell of glacier-melt river,
the sound of trees stretching to the evening.

We go rafting on Pho Chhu—it has rougher rapids,
which our guides insist will be, *"More fun than Mo Chhu."*
As we float idly down the waterway—
"Rougher during monsoon season; now it isn't monsoon season"—
we see a large, white bird take flight from a nearby tree.
It sweeps out over our heads, poops into the river, and returns home.
"White bellied heron!" Our guides exclaim. *"Very rare! Very lucky!"*
As a group we laugh—
getting lucky by watching a bird go to the bathroom seems
        only fitting
for a group of friends who have at least one affliction of food
        poisoning at all times.

Body

Earlier today, I stood in front of a mirror in a gym
filled with other bodies sweating, leaning, lifting—
I caught my freckles scattered across my cheeks
like carelessly tossed seeds: rooted and blooming.
Frowned at a pimple sprouting in the tender spot
between nose and upper lip—rubbed raw by fingers swiping
    at mucus
by the heavy touch of wind.

Earlier today, I stood in front of a mirror
in a gym filled with my body—

It is the closest I have been to a mirror since
dancing-slogging-slumping-lugging myself in and out
of tiny changing rooms to try on dress after dress this past summer.

Earlier today, I realized that I wear time on my body—
Bhutan is mapped out in a series of gnat bites:
irregular lines, the edges of mountains.
Canada rests softly against my stomach
and the undersides of my arms.
Malaysia lives in the folds of my skin
and the sharp lean of my elbows.
China hums, still, along my forearms
and down the back of my neck.

Earlier today
I stood in front of a mirror.

Last Impressions

As our final act, we—Brendan and I—build a swing on campus.
We scavenge bits of bamboo and planks of wood from the
    construction site
and carry it up the hill in the cold night air.
He has brought up rope from down in Thimphu,
and I have enough patience to stand, slowly freezing,
handing him the necessary tools.
We use a rock as a hammer
and call Nick when we cannot figure out what knot to tie.

The swing impresses itself onto me as a series of movements—
a shift in the air: once by starlight, once by sunlight.
All of us take a turn on it and scribble our names in permanent
    marker on the underside.
Over and over, we affirm: *We are here, we have been here, we will*
    be here.

Six of us leave together in a van from Ngabiphu to Paro.
We are carried in a flood of togetherness, carried by everyone who
    has yet to leave.
I find my bags whisked away from me by Kristina and Yeshey—
they are cry-smiling and insisting that I hold hands with my friends.
Oscar grabs one, and Ann the other.
Linked, we take one last walk down to the campus gate.

Five of us fly out the next morning—
Weymar bids us a goodbye in the airport.
It is rushed, and a *"see you when I see you"*
tumbles out of my mouth.

He looks me in the eye and repeats my words.
The uncertainty of the future looms in front of us.

I leave Bhutan in a series of vignettes:
the receding green of Paro's slopes,
the dragon-like clouds that gather at the tops of mountains,
the teeth of Gasa.

Bhutan leaves me too:
the words for *"good morning"* and *"no, thank you."*
At least there is no word for *"goodbye"*—
only *"lok je ge."*[61]

---

61 Dzongkha for "see you again"—the language's closest equivalent to goodbye

MYANMAR,
AN INTERLUDE

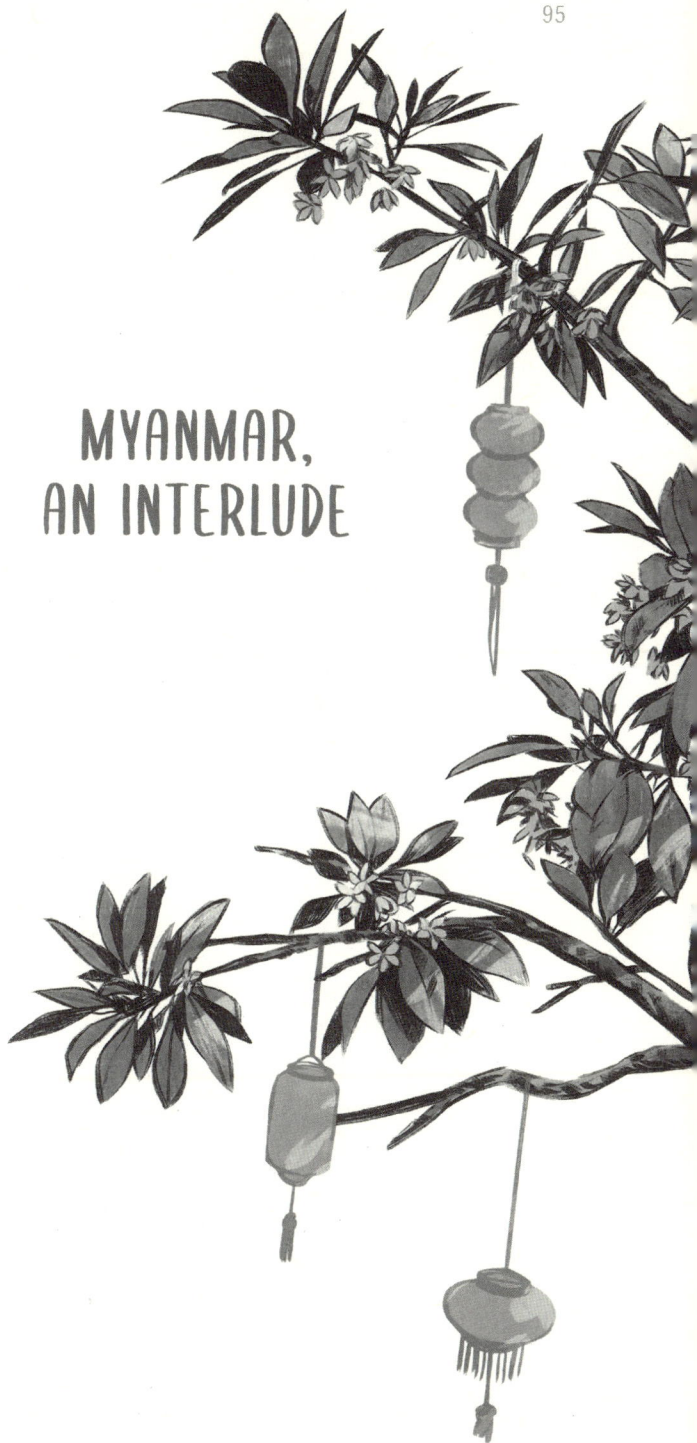

Thoughts from Places, Part One

The soundscape of Myanmar is a series of short beeps:
tapping horns that let pedestrians know—*I'm behind you.*

A red splatter on the ground catches my eye and together we
    think, *Doma?*
A short walk later, we find it: the areca nut, and neat piles of its
    accompanying betel leaf,
tiny pieces of dried coconut meat, and the lime paste.
Together, the six of us laugh because a couple of days ago, in the van
    ride from Thimphu to Paro,
we had waxed nostalgically about the distinct smell
and how we would never encounter it again—
and yet, here we are.

At sunset, Lacey, Alaina, and I wander the streets.
We are wearing borrowed shirts and flowing skirts.
We buy 600 grams of longan for 3,000 *kyats*[62]—
it is our third currency in the span of a week.
A short while later, we buy a pear half the size of our skull,
three mangosteens, and a custard apple.
My heart sings with joy as I realize that I am in a place
where I know the names of the fruits and vegetables.

All of it gets eaten as we wander the roads,
voting at each turn whether to go left, right, or straight.
Our decisions are swayed by the looks of buildings (*there's a
    beautiful blue one*),

---

62   the currency of Myanmar

and mountains of avocados, dragonfruit, passion fruit,
    and persimmons,
and the children playing in the back of a van who yell, *"Hello!"*

For a moment, as pink sunset light catches our faces
and we dodge an oncoming motorcycle, the words spill out of
    my mouth:
"I think I'm in love with this place?"
The miss and the longing for Bhutan still beats its way through every
    fiber of my being,
but the pull of tropical fruit is here and real.

In the growing evening, games of soccer and *sepak takraw*[63] spill out
    into the streets.
Groups of people crowd around a tap and pour buckets of water
    over themselves,
cooling their bodies down for the day.
The electrical wires running above our heads are zip tied together to
    create rivers of black
that pour a soft crackle above the staccato chatter of vehicles.
A fruit seller teaches me my first Burmese phrase as she hands me
a custard apple of her choice.
The one I picked would only be ready tomorrow.
"This one, though," she says as she pushes it towards me, *"is kau sau,"*[64]
I thank her and we take it, breaking the little gift into thirds a couple
    of roads away,
and spitting its black, shiny seeds off the side of the road as we cross
    a bridge over train tracks.

....

63   Known both as *sepak takraw* or "kick volleyball," the game uses a rattan ball and
    is native to Southeast Asia.
64   "Eat now."

Itinerary

This morning we learn that Myanmar is a jam-eating country. It shows up with our breakfast, and we are encouraged to ask for seconds if we need it. We eat the bread, both a little glad and a little sad about the change away from our Bhutanese fare of rice and spice.

The van pulls up in front of our hostel, and we meet Kozaw, who is our tour guide for the day. It is 9:16 a.m.

He was born in a remote village but moved to Mandalay in 2009, and before he was a tour guide, he was studying to be a Buddhist monk. *But he quit after a long while*, he tells us. He talks about Vipassana meditation and his eighty-two-year-old uncle, *who is a monk in the North*. His uncle's monastery provides food for the local people and the soldiers who don't have enough food.

When Kozaw catches sight of a heavily-dozing Rachel, he suggests that we take a nap. *The waterfall is still a long way away.*

* * *

At 10:22 a.m., we are walking up to Dee Dote lagoon. The hike up is across smooth volcanic-looking rock—elephant skin and jagged coral, bubbling red and concaving black. Kozaw notes that we're all surprisingly fit, and we exchange looks, sharing a brief nostalgia for our Himalayan home. The pools of water are colored the most beautiful blue by limestone minerals. The sun warms us all, and everything invites movement. The six of us swim in tandem, familiar with each other and the way our bodies move.

The water is cool against our hot bodies, and we crowd under the waterfall, shouting over the sound of falling water. I stretch my arms and trace iridescent lines of light up rock overhangs. Lacey leads us up a wall of bubbling rock pockmarked with holes.

Kozaw leads us further upwards and cannonball jumps himself off the overhang.

* * *

We watch the sun set for the third day in a row on the rooftop of the hostel. It is 5:54 p.m. The first star of the night winks into existence, followed by the fluorescent lights of the surrounding skyscrapers. Our hair feels strange from the minerals that now line it, but we sink into the contentment of a sun-filled day and a night that spills onwards.

Pagoda Walking

We watch the city of Mandalay stream past us on the other side of the river bank through the tinted windows of the van. Mandalay Hill rises softly out of otherwise flat ground. It is studded with white and gold pagodas, and it beckons to us from afar.

This morning, Nick, Lacey, and I walk a quarter of the way around a palace fortress. We catch sight of large-winged butterflies and turquoise-feathered birds. It doesn't cross our minds to compare this building to a *dzong*. We peek through a hole in a metal door three times our size and catch sight of trees, a man on a motorcycle, quiet air.

The fruit market tells a different story. There are weathered hands and fruit-filled rattan baskets. The three of us enlist the help of locals in order to buy our fruit. *"Eat tomorrow?"* I ask, pointing to the bananas. The fruit seller looks at me, flustered by our shared inability to understand our tongues. She's still holding the bananas out to me. The whole bunch is yellow skinned, and each one is as thick as my wrist. We're buying fruit for our eleven-hour boat ride from Mandalay to Bagan.

I throw an imploring look to a nearby shopkeeper, who laughs and says something melodic. The fruit seller ties a bit of plastic string around the stem and hangs it off my outstretched hand. *1,500*, her hands motion.

Okay, I sign back, pulling out my wallet.

* * *

We're at the White Pagoda and reading the Wikipedia page about it to educate ourselves as we walk around its perimeter. It's modeled on Mount Meru of Buddhist myth, with seven rings to represent the seven mountain ranges. We giggle a little to ourselves because we've just been in Bhutan—a land of many mountain ranges—but this pagoda is beautiful all the same.

I use the few Burmese phrases that have stayed in my head from our first night's lesson: *mingalaba, je zu ba, ayen la de* (hello, thank you, it's very beautiful).

The white paint of the main staircase has been worn away by hundreds of pairs of feet. In the little room at the top, large purple lotuses press against each other in huge heaps on plastic chairs after having been spent as offerings. Each bloom is filled with tiny bees. As I bow, the sweet, heady scent of jasmine and white jade orchids steeps my hair. String garlands of the small, pale flowers are tied above the money donation boxes. I tuck a few blue *kyats* into the slot and bow again.

Old Bagan

10:26 a.m.
We try out the e-bike on the dusty road outside of our hostel:
a series of helmet changes,
a run over plant,
a mirror shattered by a knee . . .
We decide to postpone our e-bike rides till tomorrow.

11:11 a.m.
We take a custard apple break,
spit shiny black seeds into the palms of our hands.

12:38 p.m.
Hot palm sugar coated coconut.
The squat toilet without toilet paper reminds us of Bhutan.
And there's a tree swing:
slippery plank,
rusted bike chain rope.

2:52 p.m.
Count the steps up Mount Popa.
Count the tourist's vision of Myanmar shattered—
the volcano side is littered with empty plastic
and discarded advertisements.

4:05 p.m.
We pass a field of baby sunflowers:
rings of gold that glitter and shimmer in the roadside sun.

5:12 p.m.
Blue-green roofs under a mandarin orange
in the process of sinking into the horizon.
A little boy counts out four cows walking home as we smile up
at pink clouds and a silver moon.

9:00 p.m.
Sithu greets us hello, again, and continues joking
about missing dishes, and gives us the "incorrect" juices.
We double our spring roll order, having learned from last night,
and Sithu makes sure that our pockets are full
of tamarind flakes when we leave.
The Moon Restaurant has found its way into our hearts
and our stomachs.

Homebound

The wind whips at the plastic tarp pulled tight over the steel frame roofing of the open back truck that's speeding the six of us through the dusty streets of Bagan. Along the way, Nick notes how many types of transportation we've taken in this last week: a plane from Paro to Bangkok; a car from the Bangkok airport to the hostel; the train in the form of the Bangkok Mass Transit System; a boat across the Chao Phraya River and the Irrawaddy; a *tuk tuk* through the streets of Thailand; a van through the streets of Mandalay; a special addition of a hot air balloon for Rachel, Nick, and Hannah; e-bikes to explore the pagodas of Bagan; the back of a truck in this very moment; and soon a bus from one temporary home to another.

"Don't forget our very own feet," Lacey shouts over the rushing air.

We laugh as the truck rattles and bumps its way to the outskirts of Old Bagan.

*   *   *

During golden hour, I watch the twisting arms of bougainvillea bushes grow up in spirals, dancing to the path of the ever-moving sun. The bus radio blasts Lizzo's "Truth Hurts," and I catch Rachel's eye as we start lip-synching. For a moment, we are in Thimphu and in a karaoke room with mics in hand.

A jolt of the bus brings me back, in time for the "Welcome to Mandalay" sign at the roundabout.

AUSTRALIA, AN INTERLUDE

Tourist

The word tourist pulls from the Latin word *tornare:*
to turn on a lathe, to shape wood and metal.
To be a tourist then is to be turned and shaped by the place
   you're in.

I am six, and we are traveling as a family from Sydney to Adelaide.
We are here to see things briefly, like an irregular wind.
I catch the flutter of a poster, a drive-by movie—
there is the synopsis of a book, a highlight reel.
We are turned by the pages of a guidebook,
by travel websites, by the next brightest sign.

For years after the trip, I rattle off the names of the hotels we
   stayed in.
It is a party trick that lasts for as long as I am able to hold Australia
   in my brain.
Adults are duly impressed by my memory,
by my penchant for remembering places.

I am twenty-one, and we are traveling as a pair of friends
from Sydney to wherever and back again.
The language changes quickly—
Lacey transforms me from someone who's just visiting
to a friend, to family, to someone living with her in her van, "Tabby."
As we drive from Port Macquarie to her family's home in Bellingen,
ocean air sneaks in through the open window and tangles through
   my hair.

Quickly, my understanding of geography is spun and upended—
suddenly streets and campsites crop up in my writing, alongside
      descriptions of flowers and the sky.
We take turns looking at maps and deciding which roads to
      take next,
and the names of places impress themselves onto me.
Every stop becomes the site of a new memory:
a place where we eat, or swim, or sit and read.
We choose when to move and what to see—
and yet—everything leaves its imprint.

Is it wild to think that maybe, these places are touring us
as much as we are touring them?

The sea salt, wind, and leaves that flutter through Tabby's
      open windows,
the hummus that we've bought in three different towns,
the local produce and parking spots.
Local slang has slipped its way into my speech,
taken a tour of my vocabulary and inserted bird names and trees.

Perhaps, this time, I am less a tourist
and more someone who has invited the coastlines
of New South Wales and inland Queensland to live
within and through me for a while.

Tallies

We have been to forty-one bodies of water,
twenty-seven of which have been beaches.
I have swam in twenty-four of our total number
and picked up and kept rocks from seven.

The water tumbles through my head as I sleep—
the icy morning waves of Ballina's Shelly Beach,
the quiet calm of Dangar Falls and the brackish silt of
    Brunswick River.
Each cold ocean is a relief from the salty sweat of van-packed heat.

I want to remember all of this, I keep repeating.
My journal lives in the pockets of my overalls,
or in my shorts, or in a bag hanging off my shoulder.
Worst case scenario, Lacey reminds me, *my journal is wherever the*
    van is, which means it's always near.

The real worst case scenario is that I lose the journal,
but it never goes far enough from me for that to happen.
I draw the birds we see: pelicans and masked plovers.
We catch sight of Eastern yellow robins and rainbow lorikeets.

Soon, my ears are filled with the sounds of kookaburras and
    noisy friarbirds.
I have insisted on knowing the names of things,
and now the life around me gladly begins to remind me of
    their existence.
The Eastern whipbird flits through the woods above Australian
    ground thrush.

The world breaks itself into a series of even rhythms—
Lacey and I waking up at the first light of day, with first breakfasts
of overnight oats and then second breakfasts after our
    first adventure.

We shout stories over the sound of highway wind and songs played
    on the speaker
and then whisper in the quiet
of walking through the woods or along a river bank.
We cook meals out in the open air, using our bodies as shields
    against the wind,
eating in a race against the night, or the mosquitoes.

I want to remember all of this, I say to myself as I catch things with
    pen onto paper.
Lacey and the river that we're by gets rendered in watercolor,
as does our home for the night under the flame of the forest tree.
I mark off chapters of our book as I read it aloud.

I look at the map we're using to navigate often enough to memorize
the curve of the coastline as we travel it up
and then back down again,
in our home the whole while.

Catherine Hill Beach

As we walk across the rocks to go and see the sea caves,
I tell Lacey: "*This is a good place for Big Thoughts*,"
and that "*I'm not sure yet what I mean by the phrase 'Big Thoughts*,'"
but so far, I have thought about the way sea water has carved
tables and windows into and out of rock,
about the kinetic memory of all beings—
the way even rooted and hardened vines must remember what it
    feels like
to reach and sway through empty air
and find the next point to latch onto, the next home base from
    which to grow.

I have thought about the stick of sea foam on glasses
and how salty my eyebrows feel.
About the press of rock into soft bottoms of feet,
about the stick of sand to the crevices of me,
about the thrill of jumping off big rocks to land in water.

I have thought about footprints in sand
that don't actually disappear with a sweep of a wave
because there's a layer of charcoal-colored sand
under the tan top layer.

There are thoughts about what it means to take and post
    a photograph,
about listening to music with earphones on the beach,
about the fact that I've been awake since 5:30 a.m.,
about the sand inside my bra,

about how certain overheard conversations make me feel old in
    a way
that is different from drinking tea with friends at the end of a pool
    party night.

There are thoughts about sunrises in Sungai Buloh,
about sky photos in general,
about how I am my friend Keane's word person,
about how tough the soles of my feet are getting,
about considerate people, and the shining of the sun, and
    bluebottle jellyfish.

Thoughts from Places, Part Two

Australia is a series of never-ending homes
because Tabitha travels with us the whole time.
It is an unexpected luxury to be able to call wherever we are home.
Our kitchen spills into the outdoors,
and we cook on the floor, on the gravel of a parking lot,
on a rug spread out over sand or dirt.

Lacey and I have made Thai curry and everything-into-a-pot pasta,
rice paper rolls and stir fry with *ezay*[65] flown home from Bhutan.
Cooking together is a dance we choreograph over time,
and when we cook with other people, we realize just how rhythmic
    we've become.
I pull utensils out from one drawer while she throws her weight into
    the other.

I begin chopping as she lights our tiny stove;
together, we stir and season and taste
until we know: *This will make our stomachs happy.*

On our best nights, we fall asleep to the crashing of the ocean
and wake up to the mooing of cows.
On our worst nights, the van is swarmed by mosquitoes, and
    we shut
all doors and raise the windows until there is only a hairline
    crack left—
large enough to let air in, small enough to keep mosquitoes out.

---

65   a chili paste that comes in various forms

These nights stick with us in the form of clammy sheets
and clinging clothes, but we escape as fast as we can in the mornings.
We wash our dishes and ourselves by the light of day.
There is a certain hilarity to it all—
words chopped out in gasps of laughter as we wipe our dishes
and wring out our clothes with practiced ease.

As we drive, there are sights that catch us by surprise—
a glimpse of silver trees standing waist-deep in water,
sunset light running fingers across houses,
a roadside lake full of blooming lilies.

Postcards

I find the last postcard in an op shop.
It is a photo of sunrise over Bellinger River—
a misty orange affair with the silhouettes of five birds off to the
    left side.
I buy it, and days later, on Main Beach in Foster, New South Wales,
I write a note to myself, stick a stamp onto it, and send it off.

Months later, my postcards will arrive in my home of the year.
They'll come to me from Bhutan
with images of snow-covered mountains,
and Paro and Thimphu's *dzongs*.
One comes to me from Myanmar—
posted out of Georgia—
it has pagodas appearing out of early morning clouds.

These new postcards will join the small collection of others:
a granite monolith and a blue and white teapot.
They'll be put up on a wall, all hanging from the same string.

By then, they will be well-traveled and gently-aged.
The words to myself as tender as falling asleep—
they are a bridge I build from a past (ho)me
to the one of the now.

The words become something I can share and give,
like hands and breath.
An extension of friendship,
something slow and soft.

CANADA,
AGAIN

Dreamlike

Time feels voluminous—as if I am wading through films of
	bubbled sleep.
The news is filled with stories of families separated by borders and
	microscopic bacteria.
We touch each other . . . or try to.
There's a layer between us as sheer as tulle—
clear and flimsy, but tangible.

We sit together (and by ourselves) at tables for lunch,
an eerie, impassable distance between us.
We keep six feet apart, kind of—our bodies don't know yet
what it means to lean away.
I draw a curtain around myself and minutes pass by languidly.

In my sleep, I draw close to someone I have only just met.
We haven't touched yet, but in this dream—
in this dream, we hug, and we hug as if we have hugged before.

An oil pastel scribble of mine from three years ago reads:
i want to yell that i dreamt of you.
The note makes me reckon with the distance between the now
	and then.
I don't remember anymore which *you* I am referring to in this,
and the timidity that underlies the note is gone as well—

My dreams collapse the distance that exist between me
and everything that is not-me.
They dismantle and rebuild my houses into one great home
and make it possible for me to tell everyone:
You showed up in my dream today.

Dwelling

Recently I have been asking people: *"Where do you call home?"*
The answers pour forth as they tend to, in tiny incoherent spurts.
My friends have named countries, books, and the curry their
    mothers cook.
The feeling of sitting in a field in the summer, the sensation of open
    sky and water.
They name deeper things too, like heartache and devotion,
the color yellow, *gezellig,*[66] warmth, and *saudade.*[67]

To pack in order to call a new place home, my plants have to leave
    my room first.
I clear my windowsills of aloes and split leaf philodendrons.
They gaze dolefully at me from their new dark corner as my clothes
    fold down into two suitcases,
my books into two crates.
In this move, I look critically at everything because I am suddenly
    one move closer
to The Move—the one that takes me away from this country for a
    finite forever.
Everything I own is heavier than I remember it being when
    I unpacked.

I am seized with the desire to leave it all behind.
I am reminded of what "it" all is when my postcards from
    places cascade
out of the piece of paper I have folded around them.

....

66   a Dutch word signifying coziness, belonging, togetherness
67   a Portuguese word that describes a profound nostalgia or melancholia for
    something absent

Our food encases itself too as we prepare to leave—
sandwiches come suffocated in cling film with a juice box on
    the side.
The seismically-detectable heartbeat of humanity has quieted in
    recent weeks—
we all hear the crinkle of plastic as I unwrap my lunch and crunch
through iceberg lettuce, cheese, some mustard.
The world has changed forever, and so we must respond in kind.

There is a familiar sort of comfortable exhaustion that settles over
    me as I pack—
a childhood quilt I have begun to grow into.
I sink into this moment—the security that comes from knowing:
All that I call home in this country is moving with me tomorrow.

My closet is empty, save for leftover hangers
and my set of clothes for tomorrow—
stacked as if I have a Pacific-crossing flight.

Cedar Tree

In the cedar tree today—
the one in the front yard,
the one I've been climbing every single day
since Zevon taught me
(with his eight-year-old wisdom)
how to climb cedars:
Thank the branches.
Tread them lightly.
Trust them to hold your weight—
even as you sit (sway) and listen
to the branches beneath you creak in the wind.

I am up in the cedar tree
and I have found a new sitting spot—
and if I sit still enough,
the sounds of the house wash over me.
There is the new family,
clanging pans and strumming the guitar.
Two little boys who remind me what it is like to be an older sister.
I watch them run from my new sitting spot.

In the cedar tree,
I am tucked into where
the branches meet and cross—
And if I sit still enough,
it is almost
as if I don't exist.

Minouka

Our one-block walks begin as a way to find the quiet that is missing
  in our new home.
It is the process by which we come to know the place we are
  living in:
a slow, one-step-at-a-time thing that involves the rain and
  getting lost.
The outdoors is the way we put the ever-playing records on pause,
or the sounds of the most recent home improvement project,
or the kids singing the Animaniacs country song.

We pull on our rain jackets, scarves, and boots, and step out
into the drizzle, or deluge, or the thunderstorm.
As the cats of the house make themselves at home in our rooms,
we begin to explore the woods.
We choose trails at random and see our school from a distance,
from the top of a little granite outcrop.
This far away, the buildings are composed of a series of hard angles.
I think about gentle footsteps and the muddy edges of my jeans.

The first walk is to the place where all the rocks hang out:
a little knoll in Merrill Park whose top is decorated with names of
  the neighborhood's kids.
We walk onwards, slipping on wet slopes and navigating tree roots.
The park spits us out thirteen houses away from our own.

In the most innocent and childlike of ways, we don't realize that
  these trails
have names before we walk them, for in the beginning, all we see is
  a maze.

We find a tree filled with single socks.
We talk about bringing string along to mark it as a place we have
    been before.

It is a thread that runs through all of our first walks—
but we never do bring string—
we just keep walking and it gets to the point where we
can come to a fork in the road and know:
This is where we turn to go home.

Early on, just after the world had changed forever because of a
    global pandemic,
we sit in the middle of Perth Road for a long time,
experiencing the tiny everyday magic of being still and listening.

We walk regardless of the weather—in pouring rain and hot
    summer sun.
We walk in the morning with the birds,
and the middle of the day when it is too hot for anything else to
    be moving.
We change streets and find ourselves home just in time for dinner.

Bits and pieces of the neighborhood grow prominent in our brains,
and our bodies stop having to think
about where to turn because now all of the streets make sense, and
    have names,
all of the streets have memories.

I make up a story in my head as we walk the neighborhood.
The story goes as such:
We pass the house with wisteria blooming on the outside, and the
    family living in that house
is in the front yard, or just exiting their door, and we catch eyes.

I would smile and say, "Hello."
And they would go, "You walk a lot. We've noticed you."
And we would look at each other for a moment
before I respond, with an abashed smile,
"Yeah . . . we do. We do walk a lot."

We walk until our bodies feel content and quiet enough to return
to the noise and the chaos and the warmth.
We walk until our bodies are loosened by the familiar and
    synced rhythm
of each other side by side.
We walk until we know that our bodies will recognize,
as we turn the corner, that we are going home.

The Secret Garden

We unearth the root balls of Japanese maples and hedge cedars.
We are gentle with the magnolia tree as we move her towards
   the sun.
I find a ginkgo hidden and breathless in a back corner.
We heave rhododendrons out of the way, untangling bleeding hearts
   and the ever-present periwinkle.
It is a lesson in landscaping, kind of.
Asia and Rueben teach me how to sink (propel, really) the shovel
   into the ground.
The tip of my blade encounters every rock and piece of gravel in
   the soil—
it fights me the whole way down. I jam my boot onto the step, hard,
   and sink an inch more.
Levering my grip, I heave up a new chunk of dirt and scatter soil all
   over me.
The kids grin, newly freckled and smelling of damp earth.

I learn that a cedar branch stripped of its bark is slick and cool to
   the touch.
We—the kids and I—twist the branches into a fort,
and we spend sun-soaked hours filling our lungs deep
with the smell of stories dug out from the forest and each other's
   most secret corners.

The kids bring home fistfuls of lupines, and I smell their soft green
   fragrance until my head spins.
"I think this may be my new favorite flower," I say gently,
taking a photo of the jar of them on our dining room table.

The photo jumps from me to my countries without lupines, and
    there they are planted
in the imaginations of my sisters, the imaginations of my friends.
Cottonwoods start shedding summer snow—
a wind kicks up a heaping of white tuft and swirls it around, and I
    call it *magic*.
There is a giddy new excitement to be had in every corner, around
    every block.
Suddenly, no one's garden is a stranger.
Tulips and daffodils call out to me in sunset colored delight,
and soon, so do the lilies and the crocosmia.

I learn that the flowers of the prickly barberry bush smell like
    pandan leaves
and I exult in this discovery, shoving the small bunches of the yellow
    flowers into people's noses—
*"You don't understand. This smells like home; this smells like the
    pandan leaf."*
I cradle this realization in my heart for days.

Fruiting trees and berry bushes teach me about gifts—
the gift of observation, of being willing to look and then see keenly
    where treasures are hidden;
the gift of patience, of crouching and searching as sweat trickles
    down my back
and thorns gently scratch along my forearms;
underneath that is the gift of growth, of developing fruit as leaves
    thicken under the gaze of the sun,
and stems suck up the fall of summer rain.
Deeper still—the gift of time, of the ability to wait
and trust that peas will ripen, that blackberries will swell
and darken and grow soft and shiny.

Plum trees and raspberry bushes teach me to give generously
    without fear of running out.
The summer sweetness explodes with an unthinkable happiness—
it runs down my fingers and my wrists, it spins around my tongue.

Lowell and Zevon

The kids transform the one-block walk.
In April, they collect saskies and stinging nettle,
bundles of big leaf maple blossoms and licorice root.
We make elderflower syrup and herring roe bannock for dinner.
We scoop up the fallen cherry blossom petals
and fling them at each other in a spring snowball fight.
The pink explodes above our heads, and there is laughter.

The kids delight in the Lonely Sock tree, and in return, they take us
    to The Castle.
It is a series of moss covered rocks that overlook Condor Place and
    Jay Crescent—
you get there by taking a secret path, and from that outcrop you can
    see Nch'kay.[68]
The mountain glows pink with the sunset the first time we see it,
far larger than the way it looks when it is framed in my
    bedroom window.

They teach us to tromp through muddy puddles without
    being afraid—
because there are always more clean clothes to put on,
and anyways, *it's far more fun.*
I sit and spend whole evenings taking hundreds of photos of them
    going over bike jumps.
We find flowers for the house; we encounter mysteries and
    adventures and games.

....
68   the Skwx̱wú7mesh word for Mount Garibaldi

We jump on the trampoline hidden in the woods
until our skin thrums with the feeling of tectonic uplift.
Lowell (with his eleven-year-old wisdom)
says that the feeling is like magic.
He says: *"It's a feeling that gives us the butterflies."*

Mostly, though, the kids and I play in the front yard, as and the
     neighborhood passes by
on their one-block walks.
They see me crawl out of a cedar fort half my height,
yelling for my First Mate and Mechanic.
They see us playing as the Good King, the Bad King, and the
     In-Between Queen.

The neighborhood walks by and sees all three of us up in the cedar
     tree tying bits
of frayed rope at the highest of our heights—
This is where we have been.
They see us building homes for spitbugs and watering the garden.
They see us and continue walking.

Sameness

At home, my family has a wooden picture frame that holds several
    distinct layers
of fine-grained different-colored sand pressed between sheets
    of glass,
with a series of progressively smaller camels etched onto its surface.
Led by a man wrapped in white cloth, the camels walk along the
    bottom of the picture.
As a child, I was fascinated with this desert scene and how in essence
    it stayed the same,
even if my hands were able to change it with one disorienting tilt—

The camels and the man would walk the sky,
or the rolling desert hills became jagged mountains.
Worried, wiser, and older cousins would warn me:
"Shaking it too much will ruin the sand!"
And yet, I fretted away at the picture—
smoothed the mountains into a rolling river before rushing it back
    to being a desert—
wondering, even then, how I could mimic that magic.

"You've changed so much! 长高了!"[69]
I flinch away from the acknowledgement of change—
shrinking my shoulders and ducking my head,
as if I am a turtle who can retreat into its shell.
I make myself as same-as-before as I possibly can,
disregarding forces of geography to return to a me that
    you recognize.
(Perhaps, a me you're more fond of.)

69 Zhǎng gāo le: grown bigger/taller already

At the advent of every transition,
the word "unsettled" worms its way into my writing.
It skitters across my skin and crawls along the back of my neck.
Being unsettled is to conjure up an image of camels amidst an
    indecipherable storm—
the inability to put a name to a place
is somehow the same as glimpsing something you used to know with
    a deep familiarity
from far, far away.

Recently I've been spending days by a river, watching the way
    sediment moves,
watching the tiny bits of sand dance along the firm ridges of the
    bank to the hands of the river.
I trail my fingers through the silt and learn from how quickly the
    water eddies,
swirls, and rushes into the line I create—
before continuing to dance.
I draw again a spiral this time—

And then a series of names, of hopes, of fears.
The river erases them all and sings onwards.
I scratch in my biggest, most unanswerable questions, like
what does it mean to suddenly want not to be the picture frame . . .
but the sand inside it?
The river laughs at my words—it continues to pour.

A Message

The words appear in time to my footsteps the whole way home:
Hey, this may sound really silly but can you see the sky from where
   you're at?
How the mountains look like they're punching themselves a home
out of a world of soft?
Can you see the silken oranges and the reflections of foxgloves?
I guess, what I'm really asking
is whether we're looking at the same things—the same stretch of wide
   open, spilling possibility
right above our heads.

I see signs of the same question everywhere I go—
the trails have begun to accumulate rocks covered with people's
   favorite things:
sunsets, lucky numbers, a solid teal.
None of the rocks have been moved
because we don't touch things anymore.
They're all saying the same thing: *I exist. I am here.*

Jamie

It takes a moment for the place to come rushing back to me, but it does, as steady as the sweep of rising tide. The sun glints off of water, off of the salt. The time it implies is the time we—the boy and I—decide to live by. We reset our clocks to noon. The ocean beckons.

By now, we are both shoeless—the soles of our feet meet the rise of every rock, the spine of every tree. It is a walking meditation on the question we had posed to each other earlier, one about intimacy and the land.

We don't count, or mechanize—we don't mark off the hours or pretend that there are seconds wasted. There is only the gentle acceptance of time passing as salt seeps into our clothes and heat crackles along our skin.

*   *   *

On the way to the cliffs, I find a rock. It crawls, smooth and cool, into my hand. We take one look and agree—this is a rock I have to ask the ocean permission to borrow.

I lay it by the shore and watch the water run over it with aching familiarity. I let my eyes wander, dancing across to a bit of quartz, over to a sliver of shadow, around a weighty sleet, and magnetized, I draw back, finding the first rock easily.

In that act, I know that, for right now, I have permission to borrow this rock. It slides into my pocket and sits. He grins at me because he understands, and we continue on.

This is a bit of magic, a quiet one, a shared one.

*   *   *

We touch only once, briefly—his hand to mine. But the earth holds us the whole time. We carry ourselves using the same rock, me following (clambering, really) in an unsteady path along the cliffs beside him. When we are settled, surrounded by seaside moss and lichen and cloudy towers of pink hardhack, everything is witnessed.

Without a phone, or a pen, or a piece of paper, everything registers itself on my body—from the thrill of the ocean as it carves its way up the rock face to the knowing tenderness of his eyes as he watches me complete the last of the climb. There is the tickle of lavender in my nose from where it is nested in my overalls, and the sound of an ocean in the summer—they all leave their signature.

A Body, Again

What is a body but a collection
of fleeting moments—
a series of smells, the smallest of touches?

What is my body if not the first thing that holds me,
that accepts me—that is my family?

What is my body to those who know me?
Certainly not just my stomach, or the bottom of my heel.

To the sun, my body is a place to lay freckles,
to mark the movement of itself across the sky.
To the berry bushes, my body is something to dig into—
thorn finding calf as my teeth find their fruit.

What is my body if not the one thing I carry with me at all times as
    I walk
through fear, and love, and the shapes of quiet I so dearly seek?

What is my body now to my parents?
To the people who have bathed me at birth,
who have fallen asleep with me rising and falling on their chest—
a rocking feeling, like a boat in a bay.

What is my body if not what it yearns for?
To be moving, to be braiding,
to be breathing and writing and laughing,
to be loving and loved.

What is my body if not a daughter, a sister, a friend,
    Chinese, Malaysian?
What is my body to the others that see it,
who wind their ways into it?

What is my body
if not
a home?

Bea

We walk so as to learn each other—
We have lived one street away for most of the summer,
and so we know each other's roads, each other's neighbors,
but not each other.

We embark on the one block walk.
We talk and know each other a little better.
I learn from the way she walks,
from the way she is willing to look when I point at flowers and
    the sky.

I like to think that she knows me a little better too—
in the way I know the streets
and the names of things.
As the blocks unfold, we learn about the rhythm of our runs—
eyes squeezed shut against the first of the heavy, cold autumn rains.
We run with squishy socks and exhilarated shouts and later,
when we're wringing the weather from our bodies,
we thank each other for deciding to be there for the journey.

Phone Calls

I call my mother more than I have ever called her—
We talk about the food I should make if I am feeling homesick,
like *bak kut teh*[70] (I would need the herbs to make this soup taste
  just right) or *yóu tiáo*.[71]
We talk about the garden at home and the plumeria tree.

I call my father, and he is surprised (and delighted).
We share our work days and connect, truly, for the first time.
I understand him a little better—or maybe he understands me—
now that we both have this to share.

My breath comes in puffs as I walk up the steep, secret path
from Rhum & Eigg Drive to Glacier View.
I show my father the large rainbow stretching overhead as we
  speak—as we hear each other.
I feel closer to my parents than I ever have in my whole life.

Time is crumpling in on itself—
it turns out that my mother is a geographer who asked
why in most cities, the Chinese only have one street,
and my father is someone willing to spend hours dedicating himself
  to what he does.

Sometimes, after ten o'clock, I open my window and the night air
  hurries itself into my room.
I turn off my lamp, and then I breathe—
The air smells of flowers and settling poplars and sometimes . . .

70   a pork rib dish cooked in broth with aromatic herbs
71   油条(yóu tiáo): a long strip of dough fried till it is golden

sometimes I think of telling you that I think about you in
    these moments—

about the swell of jasmine or wet city street littered
with mango blossoms,
about the feel of rushing air filled with pine needles.
Tonight, I don't feel compelled to do anything but sit and let this
    cool, clear air pour over me.

I talk to my mother. She frets over my little sisters and notes that
    I've lost weight
(which, I guess, is all to say that she's noticing, that she cares).
She asks whether I'm writing, and I say, *"Yes."*
She asks why I haven't been putting my writing online,
and I don't have the ability to explain
that my words are still being heard.

When my friends call, I find myself having to articulate my days in
    the form of stories.
I keep saying: *"I cannot wait until the day we live together again,"*
and my days can just be days instead of translations.

My mother calls, and I show her the foxgloves in the ditch across
    the road.
I show Ro Xzi the sky above Jay Crescent.
As I'm showing Tien Xzi the newly bloomed tiger lilies, my
    phone dies
and I walk home in silence.

The Mountains, Part Three

I:
>I am a too-large presence;
my feet don't quite know where to step—
I don't quite know how to hold myself.
>It is strange feeling like an impostor
in a place that asks you to be your truest self.

II:
>Sit still, let myself be eaten by mosquitoes
while painting tiger lilies and purple thistles.
Surrender.

III:
>What does it mean to be held by the earth?
The rain tumbles through the valley till the only things we see
are the stones in front of us and each other—

IV:
>So much of balance is trusting yourself.
Creek hopping, snow sliding, mountain ridge scrambling.
>Being on the moon
is louder than I thought it would be.
There is the sound of wind across glacier,
the ring of cold water down the face of the mountain.
A moment of fear kicks in and I trust myself less.
My shoes slip on the ice and the rocks, and I catch myself and
>hold still,
trying to figure out how to redistribute my weight.

V:

      The mountain mostly disappears
in a quiet cloud that listens to us listening.
Everything is a series of deep light,
except for the stuff right at our feet.

      I pray at the top—not for anything
or anyone in particular, just a steady murmur in my head
of a chant my father taught me.

      I can almost see the silent prayer stream out of me
and get carried by the wind.

On August 3rd, 2020, Jamie and I hiked Cypress Peak,
a mountain near Squamish.
It is the first mountain I have ever climbed in Canada.
I made a series of five paintings on the way up.

Yin Xzi

The everyday magic steals over me quick
as the bloom of a neighbor's delphinium.
There is always something delightful and alarming,
something humbling and beautiful.

At the start of June, I learn to walk alone.
I find myself crumpling at the sight of flowers I can no longer share
    in the now
until I become well-versed
at storing the little wonders of the walks in my head
and bringing them home as gifts, gently reintroducing the outside to
    the inside.
There aren't enough words to explain why it is miraculous to me
    that the poplar trees have bloomed,
that smoke trees waft through the air,
that the elderflower trees are fruiting—
so I repeat the facts when I can to everyone, to anyone—
I learn the call of the black-capped chickadee and sing back:
fee-bee chicka-dee-dee-dee.

One slow July afternoon, I think I am lost—
even after having walked to the point where I know
I can never truly be lost, for I have a deep confidence now in my
    sense of place—
a perturbing fear thrums high in my chest.
A walk that usually takes twenty minutes
is doubled in length as I see the tiniest of movements
and then begin to count the juvenile Western toads,
from one till two hundred and four (until I can count no more).

In watching these tiny amphibians scramble out of my way,
my fear seems incredibly small—
here are beings that have roaring, rushing giants crashing
    by overhead—
and here I am, afraid of being lost.

One August evening, everyone seems to have put themselves to
    bed early—
I walk often enough to know when moods have shifted in
    the neighborhood—
and I wind circles on the streets, avoiding linear routes.
There is something reverent about the process of learning a place
    by foot,
about going at a pace that lets you see but also encourages you
    to hear:
the squeak of a neighbor's trampoline, the steady wash of sprinklers.
Walking lets you catch the scents of dinners sneaking out windows
    and doors:
rice and curry, oven-roasted carrots.
Memories layer themselves thickly over each other.
Each corner is a site of aloneness, of togetherness, of a
    plant's growth.
The sensation of returning engraves itself deeply into my bones.

When I walk alone, everything becomes this: now.
Everything is this: here.
I have walked these streets almost every day for the better part of
    a year.
It has taught me something every single time.
I am humbled, I am grateful, I am thankful to be able to say:
This is home; I know this place.

The Big Move

In August, I am engrossed with the process of documenting the house, keenly aware of the particularities of conscious remembrance. Rendered with watercolor in my journal, the living room becomes a forever-blanket-forted space. The living room window has the outer edges of the cedar tree, the yellowing leaves of the magnolia that we transplanted in the spring, and a tiny frond of barberry. I write down that the air is filled with the sounds of Lowell and Zevon as they make a Yin-Xzi-sized entrance and make sure that the fort can *"fit three adults, or one papa."*

I paint the back porch, with my laundry on the line, as the kids paint my portrait. The siding is as close to the Stormy Maiden paint color as I can achieve. I paint Rueben in the kitchen as he cooks up a large stir fry with bok choy and black bean paste. I paint Asia at the dining table as she searches for their new house—the window-sill behind her is filled with cactuses and succulents that crowd each other.

The shelves are crammed with books, the counter covered with the kids' drawings and soon-to-be-eaten fruit. I paint Asia's vase of orange birthday lilies, games of Settlers of Catan, and the kids constructing thrones and scepters. The kitchen is rendered after every new renovation: white tile backsplash, new shelving.

Zevon asks me once, as I brush his hair, if I have enjoyed this sleepover because it's been the *"longest sleepover ever."*

I tell him, *"Yes."* I tell him, *"Of course."*

We talk about the time the three of us chased the cats Willie and Kofi around the house as they chased the American robins and Rufous hummingbirds. We talk about garden hunting for string beans and radishes, and harvesting lettuce before it bolts and turns bitter. He reminds me about looking for the good roses and the best hydrangeas and lilacs to bring into the house. I remind him of the time in which his favorite bedtime snack was oats, yogurt, and honey. He laughs and shouts that now he loves toast and butter and cinnamon.

All I can say in response is, *"I know."*

I commit it all to an unquestionably flawed memory. I paint it so that in years from now—or in weeks from now—I can look back and say: *"This is where I lived, once."*

* * *

In August, things begin disappearing. Now that the house has sold, boxes from Home Depot and Rubbermaid tubs start getting stockpiled not just in the garage, but in the spare room. Eccentric things— like the cardboard unicorn head that used to hang on the living room wall—have already spent months squirreled away, but now ordinary things start vanishing too.

The phenomenon occurs throughout the house, slowly.

It is a practice in forgetting, in letting go. It is a practice in learning the bare essentials of what you need. Zevon's favorite bowl, for example, and Lowell's favorite Hot Wheels cars.

Zevon cries when I tell him I'm leaving, moving to the neighborhood across the highway, a ten-minute drive away. I insist that it isn't really leaving, that I'll still come back for dinners and play front yard games with him.

He looks at me ruefully and mutters, *"That isn't the same. And you know it."*

Lowell accepts it solemnly, and when I paint that look, my portrait of him renders him four years older than he really is.

The day I leave, I say to the whole family, *"See you tomorrow."*

"See you tomorrow," they return.

* * *

In September, I come home to a place I have already lived in, and it is beautiful and bittersweet.

This time, when I turn the corner, there is a large moving truck parked in the driveway. Instead of a white bucket filled with oyster shells and bleached sand dollars and rosehips by the front door, there are cardboard boxes packed tight with all of the stuff that composes the home of this family.

Asia, Rueben, and I stand in the living room.

There is a moment in which we acknowledge all that has come to pass in the last five months. I eye the word "Fragile" written in capital letters across the top of several boxes and secret the familiar word into my chest. I use it to sharpen the moment and let it crack my heart wide open, ready to feel anything.

The three of us make eye contact and laughter bubbles out of my throat. The absurdity of another home being packed is not lost on me. *"Man, the kinds of things that happen when the world changes forever because of a global pandemic, huh?"*

We laugh and agree and put ourselves to work. For six hours, we are humming in movement together again. It is another lesson in land-scaping. This time, however, instead of handling the delicate roots of flowering trees, we are playing Tetris with Asia's great grandmother's dressers and her box of "Fancy-clothes-that-she-never-gets-to-wear-because-we-don't-live-in-a-city."

As we pack, I am struck by how many of the objects' stories I know—like "Books—Fantasy (Except Cherryh and Brooks)" and "Favorite bowl." I pull a pen from my pocket and write: "VERY IMPORTANT" underneath "Favorite bowl." Asia sees me doing so, and we laugh-sigh together.

We pack the plank of wood that the family uses to mark changing heights. I am there—an inch and a half below "Mama." We pack a box of "Baba's small plates," and I am there and eating buttered toast and scrambled eggs with the family on Saturday mornings. We Tetris-stack Rueben's guitars and stand carpets up inside the couch, and I am there and breathing the stifled air of a Yin-Xzi-sized-fort and listening to Rueben sing about kingfishers.

As the final act, we—Jamie, the kids, and I—carry the buckets of plants from the front yard and arrange them all on the liftgate. I find myself in the oleaster tree that I helped dig up, and the hostas that Lowell and I so carefully chose. As the secret garden rises through the air to be swept into the moving truck, I am keenly aware that I am not photographing the moment to paint it—there is no need to.

I hug each of them in turn and say, *"See you soon."*

*   *   *

In September, friends text me to ask if I am leaving Squamish in response to the photo I post of the inside of the moving truck. This is how entangled I am with this family; assumed to be a part of it even in the leaving.

Jamie and I get into his car, and we drive across the highway.

*   *   *

In the end, I come home to another place I have already lived in.

EPILOGUE

Ceremonies

We hide ourselves
in the rituals that we practice—
the way we wield knives and cook sweet potatoes
tell just as many stories as the ripening of a tomato,
or the smell of honeysuckle and black locust carried by the wind.

I spend hours raiding my journals for poetry—
reading wisps of things and hesitating my way through
    old questions,
through previous illuminating moments,
and figuring out how to speak a truth, how to let this story go.

Up on my wall in my newest home, I have hung
all of my postcards from places.
It is one of many recent attempts to return home—
to collapse the distance I have placed between me and t(here).

I return to the river, endlessly marking my constancy
against its changing tides and colors—
wade into the water and bury myself
even as the cold shocks me back into being.

The question is answered breathlessly,
has been answered for years now—
but we hide ourselves in the rituals that we practice,
and the process of expanding, of spilling out into more

is terrifying and freeing—
Write it: Yes. *Yes.*
Our rituals reveal us, they answer our calls,
and I remember my listening,
I remember the stillness—the act of sharing air,
of sharing this: *now. here. home.*

AFTERWORD

On *Home Is Here*

To write about belonging, I chose to begin with China, not because it is my place of birth, or the place I call home when I am away from it, but because it is the necessary introduction. Moving to Guangzhou, China, in 2004 was the first event that brought the notion of questioning belonging to my consciousness. In moving away from my place of birth, the next ten years of my life would instill in me a desire to understand what it means to claim to belong to a place, to claim to be a local of somewhere.

I then traveled through Malaysia, Canada, Bhutan, Myanmar, and Australia in subsequent sections of my memoir. I organized this book by place only to communicate the lessons I learned in each country and the gifts I have received in return. There was far more overlap in the years in which I have learned these lessons than the split structure my narrative implies, as I have oscillated between Malaysia and China, and Malaysia and Canada many times. Certain pieces have dates attached to them to signify that time has passed between the experience and the writing of the piece. Referring to the timeline may help you decipher the ramifications of the number of intervening years and what my memory may have done to the remembered process.

In this book, I have described the phenomenon of belonging as intimately as I know how. What this means is that my descriptions invoke sight, yes, as the sense that comes first and foremost when you close your eyes and think of a faraway place, and on top of that, taste, sound, smell, and touch. This is because belonging is something that is experienced with the whole body, not just the eyes or the heart. Each section also encapsulates a bit of my thoughts and feelings regarding how it felt to be in that particular place, how it felt to leave, to move, to return.

As I have grown up and grown increasingly more familiar with the complexities of fitting in and standing out, with the nuances of citizenship and nationality, I have found that connection comes from the telling of stories. Rephrased, the studying of belonging in academia has gifted me with insights and elucidated experiences of mine by putting words to sensations, but true feelings of belonging come when I share stories about what it means to be not-quite Asian enough and not-quite Westernized enough with the people around me. As such, I chose this format to write about belonging—a mixture of storytelling, personal narrative, and travel writing in this memoir—so that I can share what I have learned with you. Hidden throughout this memoir are lessons I have gleaned through reading scholarship but put into everyday words so that perhaps you can learn alongside me. The photographs at the back of the book are pulled directly from the stories that I've told within these pages. I hope they augment your understanding and imagination of the worlds found within my memoir, rather than detract.

Throughout the course of my memoir, I have infused Mandarin, Cantonese, Spanish, and Dzongkha when I felt that English would not coherently/completely grasp the message I wanted to convey. Where I saw fit, as you have noticed, these languages are provided with translations, either in-text or in footnotes.

In the process of writing this book, I created placeholder titles for pieces of prose or poetry—an empty bookmark for something that I wanted to include, if only such that it would not be left out. As weeks progressed, I gained perspective on the piece and realized that while these titles were a part of my story, they did not add to the narrative I wanted to convey in this memoir. It is hard, often, to let a story go and to allow the new narrative to take you someplace you hadn't expected to go.

But where does a story truly begin?

On "China"

Writing about China felt a lot like writing about a fairytale. In my teenagehood years of 2014–2016, my head transformed my homes into a place of idealized belonging. That is, I turned the sensation of belonging in China into one that wove me much deeper into my friends and network there than is truthful to the time. Much of my first year of being back in Malaysia was spent juxtaposing the displacement I felt in what my passport called home with the place in China that I felt was my true home. The short memoir that ends the section on China encapsulates the childhood fantasy I had developed over the years, pretending that I was the kind of body that could call a single place home.

If I had written about my experiences in China earlier in my life, perhaps the landscape depicted would have been filled with more people. Six years after moving away, however, the places that I called home in China have been pared down to a series of detailed vignettes. I am filled not with the particulars about my belonging in China, but a nostalgic remembrance of a time in which my belonging was assumed both on behalf of me and the people around me.

The process of writing about China was a sequence of investigative questions. I called my parents and texted friends who lived there long after I moved away, trying to piece fragments together again.

The streets I grew up on in Guangzhou have no names that I can recall—at least, not without the help of maps. Despite this, my body remembers the texture of the streets because it is the city in which I learned to ride a bike, to rollerblade, to rip stick, to climb trees, and to fall.

Precious few photographs of the four homes that we lived in over the course of ten years exist. Yet these four homes form the vast majority of the landscape that I talk about when I tell stories about China. There was house number C-17 in Golden Lake, apartments number 101 of Tower 11 and 302 of Tower 7 in Grandview Garden, and the last apartment in Dragon Pearl. The series of staircases and floors, beds and views of parks and city skyline out of windows are spaces that dominate my internal understanding of belonging in China. Here and there, the memories are dotted with people. The selection of poems in the first section speak to both of these facets of my belonging to China.

Truthfully, when I talk about my belonging to/in China, I feel that there is a distance and a disconnect. I feel too far from the landscape of my childhood to truly claim a belonging to it anymore, though the process of writing this section helped me to acknowledge that my connection to China is one that exists regardless of how far away I am from it, as my Chinese heritage and inherited rituals are rooted there. The rapid development that the city of Guangzhou has undergone has transformed my remembered place as much as my own process of recalling and remembering has done since 2014, but Guangzhou is not a place I can be without. My bond to it is necessarily written into my hair and my eyes, and it has been passed down to me through my parents. It is a bond formed in childhood that I have returned to now, with an adult's resources and insights. I wrote this section in honor of the memories that are now unremembered, in honor of the fleeting moments that still leave impressions on me, in honor of the reconstructed landscapes that are embedded in me. I wrote this to honor how, despite being away and distanced both spatially and temporally, I still belong to China.

On "Malaysia"

Malaysia is the site of the most contested of my belongings. Moving away and returning only for vacations for a decade of my life meant that I did not recognize the country as my home base, though there were houses in which I could feel at home. For the first half of my life, I felt more like a tourist in my native place than a true Malaysian. Every return from elsewhere made salient the ways in which I differed from the imagine of being Malaysian. Even worse, the fact that the "elsewhere" was the place of my ancestry only further highlighted the ways in which my Western education caused me to deviate from my Malaysian/Chinese traditions, raising unnerving questions about who I was.

As a migratory body, my understanding of my culture and my place of birth is always understood in relation to the place I am in now—the relationship is always after the break, after the move away. This opens up the space for relations to be influenced by memory, and fantasy. The notion that the processes of belonging can only become conscious after the separation is found in my own story as well. My desire to begin my story first in China (after the break from my place of birth) must imply, then, that I have an innate understanding of myself first as Malaysian, a realization that moves mountains for me, as someone who has spent many years of her life telling herself that she does not have roots in her place of birth.

At first glance, there isn't anything unusual about the frequency with which I moved between Malaysia and China, nor between Malaysia and Canada—I was an Asian body moving between Asian countries before going overseas for higher education, a common phenomenon nowadays as Western universities have a reputation for opening doors to better lives in Asia. Ethnographic studies of Malaysia, in particular ones done by Eric Thompson, show that leaving home has grown to be the expectation of many. It certainly was in my head growing up that I would always leave Malaysia for university.

Despite the growing normalcy of mobility, however, I am still struggling in the in-between—the weird and nebulous space of never quite being (t)here.

Malaysia is the place to which I have returned throughout my life. It is the place I have moved to and from the largest number of times. In many ways, even though Malaysia has shifted in and out of being my home, it has always been my center, my most consistent reference point.

On "Canada"

I struggled to write this section for quite some time—to have lived in Squamish for most of 2020 and to have formed a new understanding of how I fit into this place made it hard to look back at the things I wrote and thought two to three years ago. I wrote this explanation while sitting on a fallen log that protrudes out into the Squamish River. I was surrounded and held on all sides by the sucking, whirling, eddying glacial melt—colored gray that day in the rapidly cooling evening air of early October.

There was something about the constancy with which the river spilled, with neither a true start or end, that had allowed me to write, finally, with ease about the version of me that existed here three years ago. My words from then are filled with contradictory emotions. In them, I am content, grateful, in awe, and terrified, irritated, and off-center.

When I write about my home in Canada, it is always (and only) in reference to Squamish. Indeed the first time I named the sections of my memoir, the names first went from the scale of countries to just this town: China, Malaysia, Squamish. . . . I contemplated changing the scale of all of them—Guangzhou, Kuala Lumpur (or Sungai Buloh), Squamish—but recognized that my sense of place in the first two countries expands beyond the city in which I spent the most time. Yet, claiming to belong to Canada is far too large a mantle. It is the sweeping and crumpling of a large swathe of map, most of which remains unknown to me.

For geographical reference, however, I have chosen to stay with the scale of Canada as a place that is known in other people's understandings of the world. I insert this paragraph to acknowledge that for me, Canada is limited to the lower mainland of British Columbia, the southwestern-most province of the country.

One of my first ceremonies in Squamish introduced me to the concept of a land acknowledgement, the process of honoring the fact that this land is the unceded territories of the Sḵwx̱wú7mesh Úxwumixw (Squamish Nations) upon which we live, learn, work, and play. Hearing those words made me reflect deeply for the first time about who I was displacing by being here. It stood in stark contrast from China and Malaysia, where my belonging was defined by my right to call both countries home through nationality and ancestry.

Squamish was the first place in which I had to fight to make the places of my heritage known. The university I attended became the first place in which my Asianness was truly confronted, both among my peers and myself. Moving to a small town in the Pacific Northwest brought to light the many Chinese and Malaysian traditions that made up the core of who I am. For the first time, I felt as if I didn't fit in not because I am not Asian enough, but because I am not white enough.

Squamish is a place where I am always at the margins and the center. As an Asian, a female, a person of color, I am a body typically recognized as marginalized. Despite this, I am here in order to receive an education, I am here because I am socio-economically privileged relative to many in my place of birth, which in odd ways, places me at the center as a locus of privilege.

Much of the writing I produced in response to that is filled with anger, tempered now by time and perspective. My belonging to Canada is one I visit twice in this book because it has changed in marked ways over the course of 2017–2020.

On "Bhutan"

While living in Thimphu, Bhutan, for a little over four months, my experience was colored with a faint sense of nostalgia, as if I was returning, even though I had never been there before. My opportunity to go to the Land of the Thunder Dragon came through my university in Canada.

Recently, in a conversation with a friend, he noted how interest-
ing it is that I consider Bhutan as one of the places that I have lived.
Most exchange students, he explained, say that they've been to a
country and traveled or have been there on exchange, not that they
have lived there. There is a certain level of transience that being "on
exchange" implies that does not apply to the term "living." However,
Bhutan was a place that offered me a beautiful continuity—it was a
place in which I could blend my mountain town understanding of
the outdoors with the Asian sensibilities and traditions that I had
grown up with. I was given a place in which my own history was not
deeply entrenched, which allowed me to expand my sense of self and
experience new narratives. Perhaps, then, I wrote this as a testament
to the life I lived while I was there. There were many experiences that
prompted me to feel enmeshed with the country in a way that tran-
scended what it meant for me to be a tourist. Relative to past expe-
riences of visiting places, my time in Bhutan and the quality of my
experiences made me feel as if I was a local. My time in Bhutan, while
brief, left deep impressions on my life that I am still reflecting on.

Living at 2680 meters required acclimatization in the form of alti-
tude sickness medication and a language that sounded (as I described
in an email to a friend of mine) as a mixture of Chinese, Korean, and
Malay. Listening to Dzongkha was the first time I had encountered
a language completely unfamiliar to my ears. It was a language that
grew steadily more familiar as I learned it and began deciphering it
in songs.

Writing about Bhutan was difficult because I did not write or
journal much while in Bhutan. In part, my lack of comprehensive
journaling in Bhutan was due to an adaptation of a new philosophy of
being wholly in the moment. For most of Bhutan, I was plagued with
the worry that I wasn't sharing my experience to the best of my ability
with my friends and family outside of the country. This prompted me
to try and narrate my experiences as they were happening so that I

could tell everyone else, later. Eventually, I learned how to just be (t) here in the moment.

Writing about Bhutan involved writing just as much about the country I was in and what it taught me, as well as writing about the people I was with, a group that defined and influenced how I experienced the country. We were gifted the kind of immediate, intimate bond that comes from being strangers in a foreign land—we all shared the knowledge that we were from somewhere else.

This account of Bhutan is missing certain details, like the fact that we carried toilet paper with us wherever we went. However, I also try and avoid romanticizing the country and turning it into a Shangri-la. This is directly informed by how I experienced Bhutan both as a tourist—as someone only there for a little over four months—and as a local—due to how I looked, a phenomenon that intensified whenever I wore my *kira* or spoke in Dzongkha.

Significantly, Bhutan was the first place in which my process of belonging occurred in one compressed timeline. There was no leaving and returning, no vacillation between another "home country" and this one. My belonging and identity in Bhutan were influenced by the many countries I had encountered previously, and certainly my experiences there were held in relation to the many places of the past, but never presently so.

On "Myanmar, An Interlude"

Myanmar is not a place in which I have lived or traveled extensively—I was there for approximately six days, from December 4, 2019, till December 10, 2019. This section of the book acts more as an interlude than a section of its own.

I wanted to share Myanmar as a place that I have been in order to demonstrate how belonging is something that you can carry with you. The places called "home" as explored in "China" and "Malaysia" are a literal series of homes, filled with people who make food that

I explicitly associate with my culture(s). "Canada" pushed me to understand what it means to begin with my body as a home when the landscape around me is unfamiliar, while "Bhutan" altered my understanding of home through movement.

Myanmar is interesting because I flew into this country not with my parents or sisters, but with a group of friends carried over from Bhutan. This bubble of newly found family made me feel like I belonged the whole time that I was in Myanmar. We took to the streets with the same gusto that we had in Bhutan, trusting that we would grow familiar with the couple of blocks that stretched out in every direction from our hostel. We found restaurants we liked and then visited them twice, or three times, as if we had tested all of the restaurants in the city already and found our favorites. We made time to go slow—taking a nine-hour boat ride from Mandalay to Bagan.

After having lived in Bhutan for four and a half months, none of us felt the need to be tourists. We took an Intro to Burmese class at the hostel and chatted with shopkeepers, fruit sellers, monks. We collapsed what felt like a month's worth of becoming familiar with a place into six short days.

Some of the things that we did I can now recognize as methods by which belonging is formed: ritualizing spaces by settling in, leaving, and returning. We did this by starting and ending our journey in the same hostel in Mandalay. We ate food that reminded us of Bhutan, as well as Thailand—where we had briefly been just before Myanmar. For me, Myanmar's food also reminded me of the many other Southeast Asian countries that I had been to.

My ability to say I felt as if I belonged in Myanmar is one that I have taken a critical look at in my time since being there. I know that I come from a place of great privilege in being able to travel to this country and feel at ease. This feeling of safety comes from my own financial security and the knowledge that I have the ability to leave and from the fact that I was traveling through Myanmar with a group of North Americans and an Australian, all of whom were clearly marked as tourists.

Myanmar is not a place I call home—I don't feel able to temporally, spatially, or geographically—but it certainly felt like a home while I was in it, and that is a feeling worth exploring.

On "Australia, An Interlude"

Australia is another one of those finicky places of belonging that I thought important to add into this collection. Being the second-most recent place I have lived in/traveled through briefly this year, it taught me about another brand of belonging.

Unlike Bhutan, where my friend group and I entered without expectations or familiarities with the country or each other, and unlike Myanmar, where we entered as a group of friends but an unfamiliarity with the place, Australia was a place I traveled to in order to live with Lacey in her van for nineteen days, meaning that I was familiar with someone familiar to the place.

Lacey and I met in Bhutan a day after she landed in the country. We talked about her lavender tattoo and the identification of plants and birds and knew immediately that we would be fast friends. Upon planning for our Myanmar trip in October, I joked about going to Australia to visit her, and she joked about coming over to Malaysia for Chinese New Year.

A week later, I had my ticket to Australia booked, and Lacey began hunting for a van. On December 28, I landed in Sydney and began my nineteen-day journey. For eighteen of those days, Lacey and I lived out of her newly kitted out van—Tabitha (Tabby, for short). Much of our initial travel plans were altered by the devastating fires that raged throughout the country at the time. We altered our course to stay away from burn areas, with months of living amongst the mountains, prompting a deep desire to be near the ocean as much as possible to balance out the months we had spent without seeing a true horizon.

Australia was the place in which my journaling truly kicked off with a pocket-sized notebook that went everywhere with me. I noted street names, bodies of water, the birds we saw—there was nothing that wasn't worth recording. My geographical understanding of Australia is limited to this trip and the road trip that my family and I took when I was six, from Sydney to Adelaide (though that one is much harder for me to recall). However, seeing Australia through the eyes of Lacey taught me a lot about what it means to be a local of a place, and the little I do know of Australia's geography, I now know intimately.

Our trip along the coast of New South Wales and a bit of Queensland featured geography that Lacey grew up with, and navigating in a van taught me more street names and geographical features than I knew in my own home countries. Everything we did while living in a van and seeing sights taught me something new about what it means to be a tourist (especially with the same person across several countries), to be at home, and to know your body as a place.

On "Canada, Again"

In February of 2020, I returned to Squamish to complete the second semester of my third year at university. I moved back onto campus and became roommates with Minouka, who had also just recently returned. The two of us talked about how disorienting it was, to be back in this place that we had once called home that we now felt far away from.

In March of 2020, my university sent out an email that announced the closing of campus due to COVID-19, effective immediately. My first thought was *where am I supposed to go?*

This immediate reaction is fascinating to reflect upon in hindsight because I was not without options, or without homes. Had I reached out to my family, I could have gotten on a flight back to Malaysia. And yet, in the moment in which my university ceased being a place I could live in, my only thought was *guess I'm now homeless in Canada*.

Similar feelings rippled through the cafeteria, where many of us had congregated for dinner. Shock, disbelief, and expletives peppered the air. Canadian students were on the phones with their parents, arranging for transportation, for the immediate evacuation. Just across the border, parents in the United States of America were receiving calls from their children as well. Spurred by this, I texted not my family, but my host family.

There was a tiny quiet fear in me about the implications of texting my family before I had figured out a solution. A wild, scrambling fear that I might be stuck in Malaysia, away from this community that I had only just gotten back to, that I had already spent three quarters of a year away from.

Asia—my host mother and a tutor at the university—responded to my text about reading the email with the fact that the faculty had had a meeting about it earlier in the day. She immediately followed it up with, "*Will you be moving in with us?*"

The gladness and gratitude that flooded through me in that moment overwhelmed me—it had never occurred to me that was an option, and I told her as much. I spent the rest of March on campus, finishing off my course on rocks and losing myself in geological time, which made everything else in my life feel less consequential. Unwittingly, my prospecting about moving to the Matthews-de Groot abode convinced Minouka to decide to move with me.

On March 27, the two of us moved into the house and started April block shortly after. The two of us were taking a course that encouraged us to pick a craft and spend a month deeply engaged in the process of creating. Minouka picked cooking, and I picked embroidery. My chosen project was a series of embroidered panels that reflected on the theme of home, a particularly salient theme now that the question of whether I would be able to return to Malaysia was deeply questioned, especially at a time in which most of the globe's human population were confined to their houses. Many of the early reflective pieces of the year came about as I spent hours pulling needle through cloth, literally creating a space where my homes could exist together as I do with words now.

In May, Minouka and I took Ecological-Self and explored how we define ourselves and our relations to each other and all other living and non-living beings around us. I mention the two university courses I took in my first two months of living in the Matthews-de Groot abode because both of them greatly impacted how I thought, what I thought about, and the quality and nature of my reflections on home.

At the start of June, Minouka departed to a farm on Gabriola Island, and I spent the rest of the summer learning how to create a home by going on walks and local adventures with the Matthews-de Groot family and Jamie, another university student whom I had met in March. The year 2020 in Squamish has been centered on the creation of community and connections in the face of a global pandemic that divided me from all past semblances of home. And so, this section is filled with thoughts of the six months spent: living and walking in the Garibaldi Highlands neighborhood of Squamish, making it a home, river jumping, calling friends and family, and cooking—effectively, all of the rituals of the summer of 2020 that I did instead of writing this memoir.

On Writing

With the exception of the second "Canada" section, I wrote about my places from afar. All six other sections in this book have involved the process of breathing new life into old stories—even if they were stories I told recently, such as the ones of Bhutan, there is still a distance that they have to travel (that I have to travel) before they can feel real to me again.

"China" was a traverse through murky and half-remembered childhood memories. I wrote all of "Malaysia" in the dark, pretending that I was somewhere else. "Canada" was travelling through the past to arrive in Squamish for the first time again. I was only able to write "Bhutan" after donning my *kira* for the first time since leaving and struggled with the pinning of my *wonju* and *toego* for minutes. "Myanmar" and "Australia" were written to the soundtrack of the songs I listened to most as we traveled.

Writing "Canada, Again" mostly involved the distillation of my most recent eight months of life.

Writing "Canada, Again" mostly involved coming home again.

ACCOMPANIMENTS

ABOUT THE AUTHOR

Yin Xzi Ho (何吟曦) presently lives in Squamish, British Columbia, Canada, on the unceded and ancestral territories of the Sḵwx̱wú7mesh Úxwumixw (Squamish Nation). She is Chinese-Malaysian and enamored by the inherent rootedness and transcience of the world. During her time at university, she studied the fields of human and feminist geography, cultural anthropology, and creative writing. She loves to live and work with humans who foster growth and curiosity, and who humour her book-reading, plant-keeping, and rock-collecting habits.

Home Is Here is Yin Xzi's first book.

Printed in Canada